.

SEVEN THINGS YOU CAN'T SAY ABOUT CHINA

Also by Tom Cotton

Sacred Duty
Only the Strong

SEVEN THINGS YOU CAN'T SAY ABOUT CHINA

TOM COTTON

BROADSIDE
BOOKS

HarperCollins books may be purchased for educational, business, or sales promotional use. For information, please email the Special Markets Department at SPsales@harpercollins.com.

Broadside Books™ and the Broadside logo are trademarks of Harper-Collins Publishers.

FIRST EDITION

Designed by Michele Cameron

Library of Congress Cataloging-in-Publication Data has been applied for.

ISBN 978-0-06-339230-4

24 25 26 27 28 LBC 5 4 3 2 1

To the memory of Cowboy,
my writing companion

Contents

Contents

SEVEN THINGS YOU CAN'T SAY ABOUT CHINA

Prologue

In the earliest days of the coronavirus pandemic, before most Americans knew where Wuhan was, I had concluded that the Chinese Communist Party was lying—once again. In early 2020, China had reported an outbreak of pneumonia around Wuhan to the World Health Organization and claimed to have the outbreak under control. Yet the Chinese government continued draconian lockdowns and quarantines around Wuhan, built field hospitals from scratch, hoarded protective equipment like face masks and surgical gloves, and even operated crematoriums around the clock. Not exactly the actions of a government confident that it had the situation under control.

I used simple common sense, not scientific knowledge or classified intelligence, to answer the bell early on the Wuhan coronavirus. I've never taken the claims of Chinese Communists at face value. And when their actions contradicted their words and they started covering up important information about the outbreak, I knew they were up to no good.

Yet when I made a few commonsense observations in

those early days, you would've thought I had committed unpardonable sins based on the hysterical reactions not just from China, but also from its American apologists. At every turn, they tried to silence me and suppress my ideas.

First, I advocated for a ban on travel from China into the United States. In phone calls and letters to Trump administration officials and in public statements, I urged this commonsense step; after all, China had already imposed its own travel ban from Wuhan. But Anthony Fauci, director of the National Institute of Allergy and Infectious Diseases, criticized the proposal as "culturally insensitive," and Joe Biden denounced the ban as the product of "hysteria, xenophobia, and fearmongering" after President Trump halted travel from China. Biden and Fauci both would later reverse course. What's remarkable, though, isn't that both men were wrong—they often are—but rather that their first instinct was to leap to Communist China's defense and attack its critics. And it was far from an isolated incident.

Next, the Washington establishment rebuked me and others for calling the virus the "Wuhan coronavirus," "China virus," or "Wuhan flu." I've never understood the controversy. There's a long history of naming pandemics and viruses after the locations of suspected origin. West Nile virus, Asian flu, Hong Kong flu, Ebola, and Zika are just a few examples.

But if this custom offends Communist China, outrage follows. Centers for Disease Control and Prevention Director Robert Redfield called these terms "absolutely wrong and inappropriate." Speaker of the House Nancy Pelosi said they "make us all less safe," and Senator Chuck Schumer called them "harsh, nasty, and bigoted." Major newspapers and news networks echoed the scolding. After he became president, Joe Biden banned government employees from using these geographically accurate terms. The double standard was clear, and once again, it benefited China.

Finally, I became the first national leader to say one of the most unspeakable things about the pandemic: the virus may have escaped from a lab. Again, this commonsense observation shouldn't have been controversial. Wuhan is home to China's highest-risk "super lab," where researchers studied bat-based coronaviruses—a key researcher at the lab was literally nicknamed "the Bat Lady." Moreover, American officials had warned two years earlier about lax safety practices at the lab, which was woefully consistent with China's long history of poor lab safety and lying about public-health crises. Meanwhile, bats don't live within one hundred miles of Wuhan, and the Wuhan "wet market" didn't sell either bats or pangolins, which Chinese Communists had fingered as the culprit. Not surprisingly, a very early report by Chinese scientists found that the first known cases had not had contact with the market. In short, all the evidence from the beginning pointed to a lab leak.

Of course, Chinese Communist officials denounced me. China's ambassador to the United States condemned me as "absolutely crazy." He lectured that "it's very harmful, it's very dangerous to stir up suspicion, rumors and spread them among the people." For good measure, he disingenuously added that the theory would instigate "racial discrimination" and "xenophobia." Likewise, a top researcher at the Wuhan lab—also the secretary of the lab's Communist Party committee—huffed that I was "deliberately trying to mislead people." I expected nothing less from Chinese Communists.

But the howls of indignation were just as bad from America's elite, especially in the media. The *Washington Post*, the *New York Times*, NBC, CNN, MSNBC, and twenty-seven scientists in the prestigious medical journal *The Lancet* all condemned the lab-leak hypothesis as a "conspiracy theory." The *Huffington Post* ran a pair of articles titled "Don't Listen to Sen. Tom Cotton About Coronavirus" and "Sen. Tom Cotton Still Pitching Debunked Theory About Coronavirus." NPR declared that "virus researchers say there is virtually no chance that the new coronavirus was released as [a] result of a laboratory accident in China or anywhere else."

In their rush to attack and silence me, China's apologists threw caution, curiosity, and basic facts to the wind—which they've slowly and grudgingly come to acknowledge. About a year later, the *Washington Post* quietly edited its article titled "Tom Cotton Keeps

Repeating a Coronavirus Conspiracy Theory That Was Already Debunked," replacing "Conspiracy" and "Debunked" with, respectively, "Fringe" and "Disputed." Other news outlets added editor's notes to their articles and published soul-searching examinations about how the media had gotten the story so wrong. By 2023, the Department of Energy, the Federal Bureau of Investigation, and a former CDC director announced that they, too, suspected the pandemic had started in a lab. In 2024, even the *New York Times* published an article titled "Why the Pandemic Probably Started in a Lab, in 5 Key Points."

The Chinese Communist Party never came around, though. I continued to speak the truth about Communist China and hold it accountable in the Senate. In August 2020, China responded by imposing sanctions on me, which I still wear as a badge of honor.

These scenes from the early days of the Covid-19 pandemic reveal some broader truths about China. First, the Chinese Communist Party lies, routinely and constantly. No surprise there; Chinese Communists aren't much different from Russian Communists, who lied throughout the Cold War. But second, Communist China can reliably depend on a wide array of American apologists to defend it, far more than Soviet Russia could ever count on. These shills are everywhere: business, politics, media, Hollywood, professional sports, universities, and beyond. Third and most troubling, they don't just defend China, but also attack and try to silence its critics.

And they often succeed. Although more than three-quarters of Americans have a (justly) unfavorable view of China, they still don't often hear the full case for the crimes and wickedness of the Chinese Communist Party. China has cowed many of America's elites, celebrities, athletes, and politicians into silence. They fear losing jobs, contracts, investors, status, and worse. Better to stay silent.

These fears affect millions of normal Americans, too. If I had been a private citizen and said the same things about China that I did as a senator, my employer would've probably told me to cut it out and would've fired me if I didn't. Social media might have silenced me as well. After all, Chinese sympathizers have ruined the careers and livelihoods of many Americans for far less, provoking fear and silence across our country.

The dangerous reality is that there are some things you just can't say about China.

* * *

But I can. I'm fortunate to serve the people of Arkansas and our nation in the U.S. Senate. Our founders designed the Senate to take a long-term view; to resist

transient fads and fashionable opinions; and to over-
come threats and coercion, whether from special-interest
groups at home or foreign adversaries abroad, which is
one reason our Constitution entrusts the Senate with special responsibility for foreign policy. Put simply, I don't
fear China. I don't need China. China has no leverage or
influence with me. And I will honor the people I serve
and our founders by using the powers of my office to
speak the truth about China.

That's why I wrote this book, to tell you the truth
about China. So let me share seven things you can't say
about China.

First, China is an evil empire. The Chinese Communist Party has victimized the Chinese people for more
than a century, slaughtering tens of millions and prevent-
ing hundreds of millions more from ever being born. The
party constructed an Orwellian police state to control its
subjects, commit genocide against disfavored minorities
and destroy their way of life, torture and murder peaceful
dissidents, oppress one of the largest Christian popula-
tions on earth, and subjugate the once-free city of Hong
Kong.

Second, China is preparing for war. Former Chinese
dictator Deng Xiaoping once advised that China should
hide its strength and bide its time. No longer—China is
returning to Mao's policy of reckless aggression. It already possesses the largest military on earth and is rapidly
expanding its conventional and nuclear arsenals. All signs

now suggest that the Communists are preparing for war, namely, readying themselves to go for the jugular in Taiwan.

Third, China is waging an economic world war. It has destroyed millions of American jobs, shuttered tens of thousands of American factories, and stolen trillions of dollars' worth of American intellectual property. It has wrested whole industries from our shores and is increasingly dominating the cutting-edge technologies of the future. China is also using its vast economic power to dominate and extort countries around the world.

Fourth, China has infiltrated our society. It has weaponized its stolen wealth and captive population of one and a half billion consumers to control what Hollywood celebrities, sports stars, media moguls, college professors, and corporate executives say and think about China. In turn, it has influenced what you've heard, read, and seen for a generation.

Fifth, China has infiltrated our government. China is using both traditional spycraft and a sophisticated China Lobby to target our military, influence Washington, and subvert our state and local governments. America has failed to confront Communist China for many reasons; one reason is Beijing's corrupt influence over American public officials and their families.

Sixth, China is coming for our kids. China is buying and influencing their schools, flooding their smartphones with propaganda and filth, and killing and addicting them to the deadliest drugs ever made. Chinese communism is now one of the leading causes of addiction and death for American youth.

Seventh, China could win. A Chinese victory in the struggle with America for global mastery would start with the conquest of the strategic keystone of Taiwan and would end with the sun setting on American influence and power.

The truth about China is unsettling in part because you don't hear it much. America should've awoken to these dangers decades ago, but too many of our leaders wouldn't say what you needed to hear.

What follows is what you need to know. This book lays out the real and pressing threat from Chinese Communists based on established facts and the inherent logic of events; it's not partisan or a "yellow peril" screed. And let me stress that Chinese communism is the threat, not the ancient Chinese civilization or the Chinese people, the first and worst victims of Chinese communism.

America remains the most powerful nation on earth, but the Chinese Communist Party wants that title. The dangers have gathered, and the hour has grown late, but we can still prevail if we understand the stakes and the threat.

I'm telling you what others won't because I know you love America and want us to win.

I

IIIIIIIIIIIIIIIIIIIIIIIIIIIIII

China Is an Evil Empire

In 1983, Ronald Reagan infuriated liberal elites by calling Soviet Russia "an evil empire." How naïve! How simplistic! A *New York Times* columnist denounced Reagan's speech as "outrageous," "primitive," and "terribly dangerous."

But Reagan was right: Russian communism was "the focus of evil in the modern world." Reagan wasn't moralizing, but rather sounding an alarm. An evil empire isn't a normal nation with understandable grievances and splittable differences. By its nature, an evil empire can't be appeased, and it threatens freedom everywhere.

Today, Communist China is the focus of evil in the modern world. For seventy-five years, this evil empire has brutalized the Chinese people. Sadly, it's now the longest-ruling and most successful Communist party in history.

The party exercises absolute control over the Chinese people and will commit any atrocity to maintain power. In June 1989, the world witnessed this savagery when the party slaughtered as many as ten thousand pro-democracy demonstrators at Tiananmen Square in the heart of Beijing. The party's shock troops beat, shot, and bayoneted protesters. You probably recall the most famous image from the massacre: "Tank Man," a lone Chinese protester standing in front of a column of Chinese tanks. I was only twelve, but I vividly remember Tank Man. Sadly, his brave resistance didn't prevent a brutal, tragic massacre.

Yet the party routinely employs this same brutality against its people, even if it's not caught on camera doing so. For decades, the Chinese Communist Party has built a dystopian police state to monitor, manipulate, and master its people. It seeks to control what they see, say, and think. And what the party cannot control, it will disappear and destroy.

Just like in Reagan's time, our elites don't want anyone to say the truth: China is an evil empire, it has been so since the Chinese Communist Party seized power, and it will remain so as long as the party rules China. We'll see in later chapters how Communist China threatens America, but to understand its acts of hostility and aggression abroad, we must first understand the sinister evil in its heart. Let's start at the beginning to see how this evil empire came to power and then take a look at how the party oppresses and kills its own people to this day.

Red China: Still a Communist Dictatorship

From the start, the Chinese Communist Party has used ruthless violence to advance its radical ideology. The party's first "paramount leader"—its euphemism for "dictator"—was Mao Zedong, who surpassed even Adolf Hitler and Joseph Stalin as the worst mass murderer in history. This staggering fact is rarely heard, but it's completely true. Mao's bloody legacy continued with his successor, Deng Xiaoping, and to this day with Xi Jinping.

Violent revolution usually follows the rise of communism, and China was no different: the Chinese Civil War started in 1927, just a few years after the Soviet agents dispatched by Vladimir Lenin helped to found the Chinese Communist Party. At that time, China's government was led by the Nationalist Party, which fought Mao and other Communist rebels. The Nationalist Party dominated the battlefield initially, and by 1934 the Communists appeared on the brink of defeat. But Mao escaped and conducted a yearlong flight through China's mountains and swamps, a journey later exalted by Communist propaganda as the heroic "Long March." This brutal trek inflicted massive losses on Mao's forces, with nine-tenths either dying or deserting. Yet Mao still consolidated his hold as the revolutionary leader of the Communist Party along the way.

In 1937, Imperial Japan provoked an all-out war

against China, likely saving the Communists from defeat. Mao later thanked Japanese representatives, saying "we would still be in the mountains today" if not for the invasion. The Nationalists, as the official government of China, had to fight head-on against Japanese forces in conventional battles, while Mao and the Communist insurgents used guerrilla tactics, gained popularity, and gathered their strength.

Soon after World War II ended, the Chinese Civil War resumed. After four more years of brutal fighting and more than seven million deaths, Mao and the reinvigorated Communists—with the support of Soviet Russia—defeated the war-weary Nationalists, whose remnants fled to Taiwan in 1949. Twenty-two years on, Mao's revolution had succeeded: he seized power and founded the Communist People's Republic of China.

But the horrors of Mao's civil war paled in comparison to the terror during his rule. For more than a quarter century, Mao fanatically pursued Communist revolution through massive, centrally planned initiatives, no matter the human cost. Two such initiatives, the Great Leap Forward and the Cultural Revolution, reveal Mao as one of history's worst monsters.

In the Great Leap Forward, Mao sought to industrialize China by seizing farms for the government and starving and torturing his people. Peasants were forced to melt down farm equipment to produce steel for the state, while simultaneously being ordered to grow more food. Mao designed this policy, and local Communists enforced it, using food and terror as weapons. The Great Leap Forward resulted in the worst famine in history. Between 1959 and 1962, the famine killed up to forty-five million Chinese and drove some to cannibalism.

Four years after this catastrophe, Mao launched the Cultural Revolution to further radicalize the Communist Party and destroy any remnants of traditional Chinese society. He purged any supposed skeptic of communism and organized his most zealous followers into paramilitary groups called Red Guards, which unleashed terror across the country. As many as two million Chinese died in anarchic violence. Mao also exiled twenty million insufficiently Communist city residents to the countryside and destroyed countless historic monuments and artifacts. The Red Guards beat, tortured, and humiliated innocent civilians for crimes as innocuous as owning "old" books or harboring "old" thoughts" or even wearing eyeglasses, a supposed mark of "intellectuals." Whole libraries were burned, and most music was banned. It's hard to overstate the insanity of the Cultural Revolution. And it ended only with Mao's last breath in 1976.

Given the horrors inflicted by Mao over fifty years not only on the Chinese people, but also on his fellow senior Communist officials, some Westerners expected the party to condemn Mao after his death, just as Russian Communists had denounced Stalin after he died. On the contrary, the party deified Mao and still does today. And the violence and terror continued.

Deng Xiaoping, who ultimately succeeded Mao as the paramount leader, explained the party's logic: "Our evaluation of comrade Mao Zedong . . . is not about the person of Mao Zedong alone, *it is inseparable from the entire history of our party*. . . . To blacken Mao is to blacken our country" (emphasis mine). The party didn't even literally bury Mao, but rather embalmed his body, which it displays to this day in a grand Beijing mausoleum. Mao's giant portrait still hangs in Tiananmen Square, and the Chinese currency bears his face.

Without Mao, there would be no Chinese Communist Party. And just as his body and portrait remain in the heart of the capital, so his memory and murderous ideology remain at the heart of the party.

Yet many outsiders delude themselves about the nature of Chinese communism by peddling a myth about "moderate Communists." Western observers have long suggested that Deng and his successors renounced Mao, abandoned communism, and in effect became capitalists along the way. According to President Jimmy Carter, for example, "Deng Xiaoping wanted to open China with more human rights and freedom for the people" and "China has become a very open economic system because of Deng Xiaoping." Unfortunately, such illusions have led American policymakers astray for decades. At most, the Communist Party shifted tactics after Mao's death as it moved from a revolutionary party to an established ruling party perpetuating its own dictatorial power.

Consider, for instance, the barbaric One Child Policy, which prohibited Chinese women from having more than one baby. In the name of population reduction, the Communist Party extended its gruesome reach all the way inside the family—an ultimate ambition of totalitarian rule. China enforced the policy through forced abortions, involuntary insertion of contraceptive devices, and sterilization. The One Child Policy and associated measures led to more than 330 million abortions and approximately 200 million sterilizations. And this policy started three years after Mao's death and continued for nearly four decades—hardly the mark of a reformed, post-Mao, "moderate" Communist Party.

The "moderate Communist" myth owes much to the friendly façade of the elfin Deng. Upon taking power, he famously declared a new era of "reform and opening up." And it's true that the party reduced the disastrous central planning of the Mao era and adopted some market reforms, such as allowing foreign investment into China. But these reforms weren't designed to transform China into a capitalist democracy or to improve the lives of normal Chinese, but rather to cement the Chinese Communist Party's power. As Deng put it, the party would place "Capitalist Tools in Socialist Hands."

From the beginning, Deng tolerated no dissent about

the Communist Party's authority, Marxism, and socialism. Even as he adopted some economic reforms, Deng
reassured his fellow Communists that "political power is
in our hands." As for political reform, Deng believed that
"we should not only talk about using dictatorial means,
we should be ready actually to use them" to maintain
power. And Deng did use such means: he was behind
the massacre of pro-democracy demonstrators in Tiananmen Square in 1989, having accused them of trying
to subvert the party and declaring "we cannot let them
have their way." In that blood-soaked square, Deng and
his fellow Communists demonstrated that they might
welcome Western money but never Western ideas—
even as too many Western leaders willfully blinded
themselves to this lesson.

As when Mao died, China remained an evil empire
after Deng left power. His successor, Jiang Zemin, continued the party's practice of employing market-based
methods in service of Communist ideology. But he condemned the "capitalist sham of 'democracy,' 'freedom,'
and 'human rights'" and warned that "the Western model
of politics must never be copied." As Jiang watched communism collapse in Russia, he resolved to avoid that fate
in China. "The end of the Cold War and the demise of
the Soviet Union gave us a lot of insight," Jiang observed.
"We did not lower the banner of Marxism; rather, we
more firmly resolved to uphold Marxism-Leninism and
the leadership of the Chinese Communist Party."

And this commitment to communism remains today. Xi Jinping, China's current paramount leader, demonstrates the continued preeminence of Communist ideology. Indeed, Xi has a doctorate in Marxism-Leninism. Amid a sense that too many party officials had grown corrupt and insufficiently passionate about Marxism, Xi became party general secretary in 2012. In an early speech, he stressed that "our Party has always emphasized adherence to the basic principles of scientific socialism." He credited "Marxism-Leninism and Mao Zedong Thought" with the rise and strength of modern China. Xi has also declared that "history and reality tell us that only socialism can save China." In 2018, Xi celebrated Karl Marx's two hundredth birthday by declaring the author of *The Communist Manifesto* "the greatest thinker of modern times." He still blames the fall of the Soviet Union on its abandonment of Lenin, Stalin, and Communist ideology: "If we had completely abandoned Mao, the way the Soviet Union abandoned Stalin, we would no longer be in power today." And Xi has collected this stew of Communist ideology into what's known as "Xi Jinping Thought," which in 2017 the party added to its constitution.

Xi's actions have matched his words. Upon taking power, Xi launched a sprawling purge that would have made Lenin and Stalin proud, and these periodic purges continue to this day. He has developed a Mao-like cult of personality in popular culture. For example, the party has released Xi's "Little Red App," which quizzes users on Communist ideology and gives them access to Xi's essays and other Marxist classics; in less than a year, the app had more than one hundred million downloads. The party also eliminated term limits for president to allow Xi to serve for life. Xi has cracked down on powerful businessmen like Jack Ma, driving the celebrity billionaire into virtual seclusion after Ma criticized government officials. Xi also reasserted party control over "private" businesses and further empowered state-owned and state-affiliated enterprises.

It's not surprising that Xi is often called the most powerful and dangerous Chinese leader since Mao. What's surprising is that, despite a century of the party's brutal and bloody history, so many Western leaders and elite can't accept that China remains an evil Communist dictatorship. After all, many of the horrors of Chinese communism aren't found in history books, but rather are taking place as you read this book.

Techno-Totalitarian Police State

In some ways, the Chinese Communist Party today wields more power and more total control than it did in the second half of the last century. Indeed, Xi may well be more powerful than Mao, who could only dream of the advanced technological tools in the hands of

Xi's Communist Party. The party's eyes and ears are everywhere, always watching and eavesdropping on the greatest threat to its rule: the Chinese people.

China has vastly increased the spending on its military, but the government still spends as much money on controlling its own people as it does on its military. When paired with regional and local governments, the party has built a police state from the pages of George Orwell's *1984*. Today, 2 million police officers monitor China's streets, supported by an estimated 3.5 million private security officers and 660,000 paramilitary soldiers in the People's Armed Police.

This police state pursues a single-minded, unmistakable Communist goal: total control. Every police officer pledges to "firmly uphold the absolute leadership of the Chinese Communist Party." One of the People's Liberation Army's missions is to "consolidate the leadership of the Communist Party of China and the socialist system." Xi Jinping has referred to his security services as "the knife handle" of state control—with the knife's handle held by the party and the blade against the throat of the Chinese people.

As an average Chinese person walks through his city or drives home from work, it's not just the police he passes every day; it's also the cameras, everywhere. More than half the world's nearly one billion surveillance cameras are in China, powered by the world's most advanced artificial intelligence and facial-recognition software. The party claims that the nation's cameras can identify any of China's 1.4 billion subjects in a single second.

And there's no escape from the real world into the digital world; if anything, the Communist Party controls cyberspace even more completely. For years, the party has built what has become known as "the Great Firewall" to achieve its goal of a "secure and controllable internet." China deploys more than two million internet censors to guard this Great Firewall. Chinese censors delete billions of posts that don't comply with Communist ideology. When the party eliminated presidential term limits so Xi could hold that office for life, they banned the phrase "I don't agree." Around each anniversary of the Tiananmen Square Massacre, censors add "that year" and "that day" to the list of banned words, along with references to "June 4." The party can even monitor private conversations on apps like WeChat, automatically deleting or changing words without notifying the sender.

Any written criticism of the party, online or in print, could get the Chinese author fired, harassed, or jailed. As a result of this unrelenting pressure, China's writers and moral voices not only are censored by the state, but also censor themselves. The award-winning Chinese author Murong Xuecun said of his writing that "I am a proactive eunuch, I castrate myself even before the surgeon raises his scalpel." But even that's not enough: he still fled China into exile.

When someone gets out of line, the party doesn't need

to do much investigating—China's laws are intentionally vague to chill dissent and turn everyone into a criminal-in-waiting. And with a conviction rate over 99.9 percent, punishment isn't in doubt.

But the party doesn't even have to arrest or imprison its subjects to ruin them. The party has experimented with a more insidious form of control called a social-credit score. While a credit score in the United States measures financial reliability, China's social-credit score would measure political reliability. What's more, a low social-credit score would affect a person's ability not only to get a loan, but also to obtain a job, purchase train tickets, or travel overseas. In 2019 alone, the party blocked at least thirty million plane and high-speed train ticket purchases by individuals with low social-credit scores.

Orwell likened totalitarian government to "a boot stamping on the human face—forever." In Communist China, one could add "a smartphone app monitoring your face—forever." And while every Chinese subject lives under this police state, some disfavored groups suffer even more brutal treatment.

Christian Persecution

Surprisingly to many, China has one of the world's largest Christian communities, hence also the world's largest oppressed Christian population. Some seventy to one hundred million Chinese Christians—nearly as large as the Chinese Communist Party itself—suffer under Communist rule, a remarkable testament to the faith of these harassed, marginalized, and abused believers.

Chinese Christians must practice their faith either with strict party scrutiny or illegally. Under Chinese law, churches must register with the government and accept party-approved clergy. The Chinese flag flies over registered churches, which must surrender their membership lists to the government and allow the party to censor sermons and other teachings. For the Catholic Church, the party selected "bishops" without the Pope's approval for decades and still retains outsize influence over bishop selections under a secret agreement from 2018 with Pope Francis. Adding insult to injury, the Pope also agreed to legitimize Chinese bishops whom the Church had previously excommunicated.

Tens of millions of Chinese Christians refuse to bow to Communist regulation of their faith; at least half of China's Christians worship in unregistered churches. Beijing alone hosts an estimated two thousand "house churches," proving once again that mortal tyrants—whether Caesar's legions or Xi's thought police—cannot silence His Word.

But the Communist Party certainly tries, with fines, evictions, imprisonment, and outright destruction of these unregistered churches. In 2016, a Chinese demolition crew buried a pastor and his wife alive when they tried to stop a bulldozer from destroying their unregistered church—the pastor's wife tragically suffocated to death under the rubble. Unregistered Christians have reportedly faced arrest and imprisonment in "transformation" or "reform" facilities, where they are beaten and mentally tortured until they "admit their mistakes." Some firsthand accounts even indicate that unregistered Christians have been sent to concentration camps.

Xi Jinping has intensified the party's anti-Christian crusade in recent years, banning kids from attending church, eliminating Sunday schools, and requiring schoolchildren to sign pledges to remain atheist—a clear attempt to wipe out Christianity among the next generation. The party has also banned online retailers in China from selling the Bible, torn down thousands of crosses in public areas, and demolished an untold and growing number of churches. Party members have forced Christians to replace images of Jesus and Mary with portraits of Xi. Local Communist bosses have even banned Christmas decorations and celebrations.

The party doesn't merely persecute Christians: it aims to corrupt and blaspheme the faith from within. The party is literally *rewriting* the Bible and hopes to publish by 2029 a new "translation" that will replace the Word of God with the word of Mao. For example, in John 8:7–11, Jesus is asked if a woman should be stoned for the crime of adultery. He replies, "He that is without sin among you, let him first cast a stone at her." The crowd disperses, and Jesus then says to the woman, "Go, and sin no more." But in the Communist version, Jesus waits until the crowd leaves and then stones the woman himself, explaining, "I too am a sinner. But if the law could only be executed by men without blemish, the law would be dead." Whether you're a Christian or not, such blasphemy is stomach-turning. For Communists, nothing is sacred.

In America, all men are equal under the law because all men are equal before God. For Communists, there is no human equality because there is no God. Under communism, the value of a human life depends on its usefulness to the party.

The party sees Christians as a threat and therefore persecutes them. Yet, perhaps because Chinese Christians belong to the world's largest faith community and have powerful outside advocates, the party's persecution of them is mild compared to how it represses groups like the Falun Gong, Tibetans, and Uyghur Muslims, whom it perceives as even greater threats.

Falun Gong and the Price of Dissent

Falun Gong, a Chinese spiritual movement founded in 1992, draws inspiration from traditional Chinese culture and Buddhism and emphasizes the tenets of "truthfulness, compassion, and forbearance"—all despised by the Chinese Communist Party. You may recognize its adherents from their meditation and breathing exercises in public parks. Like Christianity in China today, the number of Falun Gong once approached the official membership of the Communist Party, with an estimated seventy to one hundred million practitioners. As this new spiritual movement spread, it did so largely unimpeded by the Communist Party, which initially sensed no threat from it.

But everything changed in 1999, when thousands of mostly older Falun Gong practitioners held a peaceful, orderly, and quiet protest outside a Communist Party compound. After several hours, the protesters dispersed as calmly as they had arrived. The gathering caught China's rulers by complete surprise, however, panicking and enraging party leaders, who were incensed that a group outside the party could grow so large and then challenge the party's authority and Communist ideology.

Within weeks of the protest, the party labeled Falun Gong an "evil cult" and then–General Secretary Jiang Zemin ordered a campaign to "disintegrate" the movement. According to one report, Jiang declared that "beating them to death is nothing. If they are disabled from the beating, it counts as their injuring themselves. If they die, it counts as suicide!" The party also formed a special security agency with the mission to destroy Falun Gong without regard for the law.

The party has pursued this mission with depraved zeal. China's police and security forces have rounded up hundreds of thousands of Falun Gong practitioners and leaders, throwing them in prison and forced-labor camps. Guards torture these prisoners, shocking them with high-voltage electric batons until their entire bodies are burned and depriving them of food, water, and sleep.

And in an act of utter barbarism, the party also forcibly harvests the organs of Falun Gong prisoners. According to the congressionally chartered Victims of Communism Memorial Foundation, China suspiciously saw more than triple the number of hospitals performing transplant surgeries shortly after the crackdown began, enabling an increase in kidney transplants by more than 500 percent, heart transplants by 1,100 percent, liver transplants more than 1,800 percent, and lung transplants by nearly 2,500 percent. In just the first decade of the party's war against Falun Gong, it killed an estimated 65,000 practitioners for their organs. Medical analysis suggests that the party even harvests organs from living prisoners, effectively executing them by heart transplant. To top it off, this gruesome practice earns the party around a billion dollars a year.

The party has largely succeeded in "disintegrating" Falun Gong: the movement has shrunk to an estimated seven to twenty million adherents. In an infamous interview with *60 Minutes* a year into the crackdown, Jiang smirked when asked about it and said, "No Falun Gong followers have ever been sentenced to death." Perhaps not "sentenced," but millions have been condemned to harassment, imprisonment, torture, and murder for the grave sin of peacefully protesting in China.

That is the price of dissent under Communist rule.

Tibet: Slow-Motion Genocide

Before the Falun Gong movement, there was Tibet. As soon as the Chinese Communist Party seized power in 1949, it targeted Tibet for conquest. Mao began a genocidal campaign to erase the Tibetan way of life, a campaign that continues to this day.

Tibet is a vast land atop the world's highest plateau in the shadows of the Himalayan Mountains in remote Southwestern China. The region is larger than California and Texas combined, yet home to barely more people than metropolitan San Diego. Given its forbidding geography and small population, Tibet developed a distinctive language, religion, and culture in relative isolation, while also maintaining significant autonomy from Imperial China. After the last Chinese dynasty collapsed, Tibet achieved de facto independence from the new Republic of China in 1912 under the temporal rule of the Dalai Lama, the spiritual leader of Tibetan Buddhism.

But Mao brought Tibet to heel. He asserted Communist sovereignty over lands once controlled by Imperial
China, no matter how long ago. He also saw Tibet as
a buffer zone against South and Central Asia and an
important source of China's water supply and other natural resources. With Mao's patron, Joseph Stalin, urging
him to strike fast, the Chinese Communists invaded
Tibet barely a year after taking power. The Dalai Lama's
government signed an annexation agreement with Mao,
establishing Chinese sovereignty over Tibet, that also
promised religious freedom and political and cultural
autonomy.

As usual, Mao lied. The Communists gradually
strengthened their grip on Tibet. In 1954, Mao hinted
at his true feelings toward Tibetan Buddhists, telling the
Dalai Lama that "religion is poison." By 1959, fearing
total Communist domination and starvation during the
Great Leap Forward, some Tibetans rebelled, and the
Dalai Lama repudiated the annexation agreement. But
the Communist forces quickly defeated the Tibetans, and
the Dalai Lama fled to India, where he remains today.

Ever since, the party has conducted a slow-motion
genocide against Tibetans and their culture. The Communists destroyed monasteries, devastated the population
of Tibetan monks, and jailed as many as one in five
Tibetans. The Tibetan government-in-exile estimates that
Communist authorities killed 1.2 million Tibetans by
1979—an obscene death toll for such a small population.

The living are subjected to propaganda, reeducation, harassment, arbitrary arrest, and torture.

And just as the Communists are desecrating the Bible, they're also corrupting the traditions of Tibetan Buddhism. In 1995, for instance, the Dalai Lama proclaimed a six-year-old boy to be the reincarnation of the Panchen Lama, the second holiest man in Tibetan Buddhism. Just days later, the Communists disappeared the boy and his family and selected their own Panchen Lama. The boy has never been seen since. Worse still, the party intends to take similar actions when the Dalai Lama dies; one Communist official has laughably claimed that "reincarnation of living Buddhas, including the Dalai Lama, must comply with Chinese laws and regulations."

China is also ethnically cleansing Tibet. The party sends thousands of ethnic Chinese to Tibet to dilute the local culture and removes Tibetans from their own land. For example, the party has placed at least 15 percent of Tibetans into forced-work training programs and then shipped "graduates" to different parts of China. In recent years, the party has forced more than three-quarters of Tibetan children into boarding schools away from their families to destroy Tibetan culture and language among the young.

In the ultimate act of protest of Communist repression, more than 150 Tibetans have burned themselves alive over the last fifteen years. The party's response was to dispatch a notorious and brutal party boss, Chen Quanguo. He set about laying an "inescapable net" across Tibet, bringing tens of thousands of party members to the region, building hundreds of police stations, and forcing thousands of Tibetans into "reeducation" classes. Chen's "net" of police stations slashed response times and allowed police officers armed with fire extinguishers to stop dozens of these self-immolations, which had embarrassed the party. His police then interrogated and tormented the burned survivors.

President Kennedy memorably said of the Berlin Wall that "freedom has many difficulties and democracy is not perfect, but we have never had to put a wall up to keep our people in." Likewise, we've also never had to build police stations to stop our people from burning themselves alive.

Uyghurs: Genocide on Fast-Forward

What the Chinese Communist Party has done to Tibet for seventy years has been put on fast-forward in Xinjiang over the last decade. Xi Jinping has unleashed on this autonomous region what he's called the "organs of dictatorship" to conduct a genocide against the Uyghur people.

Xinjiang is a huge, remote province in Northwestern China, nearly as large as Alaska—one-sixth of all China—but home to only twenty-five million people, including more than eleven million Uyghurs. The Uyghurs are a Muslim people of Turkish descent with a distinctive culture, history, and language. As with the Tibetans, this distinctiveness has long aroused suspicion from the Chinese Communist Party. And like Tibet, Xinjiang is an important buffer zone against the turmoil of Central Asia and is rich with natural resources.

From the beginning, Mao and the Communists sought to ethnically cleanse the province. The party settled millions of ethnic Chinese—as Stalin himself suggested to Mao—and relegated Uyghurs to second-class status, causing inevitable tensions between the two groups. Protests occurred on both sides that at times turned into riots, followed by police crackdowns and violent reprisals by Uyghurs—some real, others fabricated by Communist authorities.

Shortly after taking power, Xi accelerated Communist repression of the Uyghurs into a genocidal campaign. He instructed local authorities to show "absolutely no mercy," and the party started building concentration camps. Then, a few years later, Xi reassigned to Xinjiang none other than Chen Quanguo, who imported the brutal tactics he had perfected in Tibet. Chen massively expanded the concentration camps and initiated the systematic genocide of Uyghur culture, as described in Nury Turkel's chilling book, *No Escape: The True Story of China's Genocide of the Uyghurs*. As Chen put it, he was there to "gnaw bones."

Though cloaked in Communist secrecy, life inside the concentration camps is hell on earth, according to accounts that have leaked out. Most sources estimate that the party has interned at least two million people, mostly Uyghurs, in these camps, though some believe the number is closer to three million. Survivors explain that the main objective of the camps is to brainwash the Uyghurs and destroy the Uyghur way of life. The guards beat, torture, starve, and gang-rape prisoners to force them to submit—and they murder those who don't. And to wipe out the next generation of Uyghurs, the party uses forced sterilization and insertion of contraceptive devices. This policy is succeeding: between 2017 and 2019, the Communists slashed Xinjiang's birthrate in half.

The party is simultaneously destroying Uyghur culture outside the camps. Communist enforcers have desecrated more than three-quarters of the mosques in Xinjiang, confiscated religious items from private homes, and even bulldozed Muslim graveyards. When not interning Uyghurs in concentration camps, the party enslaves thousands of Uyghurs in factories around China. Outside China, Communist agents harass the Uyghur diaspora, pressuring them to return to Xinjiang by threatening their relatives.

Xinjiang also is the testing ground for the party's techno-totalitarian police tactics, giving it control over the daily lives of Uyghurs unseen in the lamentable history of tyranny. In his first two years, Chen blanketed

Xinjiang with more than 7,700 police stations, millions of surveillance cameras with facial-recognition software, and countless checkpoints. Under Chen's orders, authorities also take blood and hair samples from Uyghurs, along with fingerprints, voice samples, and face scans. They feed all this information into their artificial-intelligence systems, which they boast can produce the names of tens of thousands of suspicious Uyghurs to be rounded up and thrown into camps.

Leaving nothing to chance, the party employs old-fashioned spying techniques as well. The "Becoming Family" initiative, for instance, is especially invasive. This program has forced Uyghur families to welcome more than one million Chinese outsiders into their homes. Uyghur households must provide food, bedding, and other accommodation for these live-in spies, who monitor the Uyghurs' behavior, search their homes for incriminating materials, and even recruit their kids to inform on their parents. Terribly but unsurprisingly, these live-in spies often become live-in sexual predators, too.

The party also takes extreme measures to leave the Uyghurs defenseless against these abuses. As in all of China, of course, gun ownership is strictly prohibited. Uyghur families can keep only two knives in their homes: one small vegetable knife and one larger knife (often a meat cleaver). Both knives carry QR barcodes for tracking, and the larger knife must be chained to the kitchen counter.

In *No Escape*, Nury Turkel retells the story of Communist officials forcing a group of Uyghurs around the Chinese flag, where a voice over a loudspeaker bellows the question "Is there a God?" The terrified Uyghurs answer no. The voice then asks, "Who is your new God?" The Uyghurs compliantly answer, "Xi Jinping." This is the devastating purpose of the Uyghur genocide.

Hong Kong Oppression

Chinese Communists aren't just tightening their grip on places like Tibet and Xinjiang, but are also extending their reach to new lands.

Hong Kong, a vibrant international city of seven million people on the southern coast of China, was long the last bastion of freedom on mainland China. It became a British colony in the nineteenth century and benefited immensely from British institutions like the rule of law and the free-enterprise system. As a result, Hong Kong transformed into an industrial powerhouse and then a global center of commerce and finance. Though never a pure democracy, the city enjoyed autonomy and widespread economic, civil, and political freedoms.

All that began to change as Great Britain's ninety-nine-year lease on large parts of Hong Kong's territory approached its expiration date in 1997. British prime minister Margaret Thatcher had little leverage in negotiations with Deng Xiaoping and felt compelled under threat of war to turn over all of Hong Kong. Nevertheless she secured the Chinese Communists' commitment to govern Hong Kong under a "one country, two systems" principle and to preserve Hong Kong liberties after China reclaimed sovereignty. Deng further promised that China would maintain Hong Kong's autonomy for at least fifty years. He even celebrated the agreement with a speech titled "China Will Always Keep Its Promises."

On the contrary, Chinese Communists always break their promises. At first, though, Hong Kong's democratic spirit thwarted Communist efforts to subjugate the city. In 2003, China's puppets in Hong Kong's government proposed a vague "national security law" that threatened the traditional rights of Hong Kongers. The law seemed likely to pass, but something then happened that never could have happened in China: hundreds of thousands of Hong Kongers took to the streets in protest. The protests staggered the unpopular Hong Kong government, which shelved the law. This dynamic played out again in 2012, when Hong Kong's government proposed a "Moral and National Education" plan to indoctrinate Hong Kong kids with Communist propaganda. Again, thousands of Hong Kongers took to the streets, and again the government backed down.

But this pattern of hesitation and equivocation ended when Xi Jinping took power. In 2014, the party unveiled a new election law that gave Beijing effective control over who could run for the city's top office. Hong Kongers again poured into the streets, this time demanding full democracy and shutting down parts of the city for months. Pro-democracy demonstrators used umbrellas as shields against pepper spray and tear gas, earning a plucky nickname for their bravery: "the Umbrella Movement." Yet the party didn't back down this time, ultimately taking control of "elections" for Hong Kong's top office.

In 2019, Hong Kongers won a final—but temporary—victory against the Communists when they defeated a proposed Hong Kong extradition law that would have allowed China's Communist Party–aligned courts to extradite anyone wanted by the Chinese Communist Party for trial in mainland China. This time, millions of demonstrators marched in the streets for months in one of the largest protests in Hong Kong's history. For a third time, the Communist Party's puppets in Hong Kong's government buckled under the pressure. Tragically, this victory was short-lived.

Xi had seen enough and took matters into his own hands. In 2020, under cover of the coronavirus pandemic, Beijing bypassed Hong Kong's government entirely and imposed a sweeping national-security law on the city. In purposely vague language, the law criminalizes normal acts of free expression, assembly, and association. These "crimes" carry draconian punishments of up to life in prison, while Hong Kongers are allowed to be tried in Chinese courts. And the law created powerful security forces in Hong Kong, answerable only to the party.

Since 2020, the party has used the security law to silence dissent and effectively to eliminate the pro-democracy opposition. The Umbrella Movement's activists have fled into exile or left public life—or been thrown in jail. Independent newspapers and websites have been closed and had their assets seized. Students suffer through Communist indoctrination. Neighbors inform on neighbors. The Communist Party is systematically destroying Hong Kong's civic culture and institutions. And in 2024, Hong Kong's puppet legislature finally passed the city's own national-security law, which in the past would've prompted outcries from the civilized world as a deadly threat to Hong Kong's autonomy and freedoms. Instead, the world simply shrugged, because you can't kill what's already dead.

For more than 150 years, Hong Kong enjoyed the blessings of freedom. Chinese Communists promised at least another fifty years of freedom, yet reneged in less than half that time. Now Hong Kong's seven million souls are suffering the fate of the Uyghurs, Tibetans, and more than a billion Chinese condemned to live under the yoke of the evil Chinese Communist Party.

* * *

Though Hong Kongers are the first victims of Chinese conquest in the twenty-first century, they may not be the last. The national-security law, on its own terms, applies to offenses committed "from outside the Region by a person who is not a permanent resident of the Region." In other words, the party didn't write a regional or a national law—it wrote a global law. With the stroke of a pen, it purported to extend the walls of its newly imprisoned city to encompass the whole world. Barely a month later, authorities issued their first warrant for an American citizen for violating the new law.

A party that writes tyrannical global laws has global ambitions. And the surest way to achieve global ambitions is to build a world-class military—which, as we'll see next, is exactly what the Chinese Communist Party is doing.

II.

China Is Preparing for War

During his celebrated visit to China in 1972, President Richard Nixon confided to his diary that Communist China could become "the most formidable enemy that has ever existed in the history of the world." Nixon's dark forecast has arrived.

As the Chinese Communist Party has grown more repressive at home, it has grown more aggressive abroad. China has undertaken the largest peacetime military buildup in history, amassing the biggest and second most advanced armed forces in the world. China has claimed hundreds of thousands of square miles of ocean, built and militarized artificial islands, and expanded its overseas military presence. Chinese Communists now openly threaten war against Taiwan.

In 2021, Xi Jinping marked the party's hundredth anniversary by declaring that his international foes "will have their heads bashed bloody against a Great Wall of steel forged by over 1.4 billion Chinese people." Xi has also reminded his military leadership that the "laws of the jungle" govern international competition.

Of course, the Communist Party's aggressive actions and rhetoric aren't surprising. The party has a long history of aggression resulting in death and horrific suffering for millions. As former U.S. State Department official and China expert Miles Yu put it, "The Beijing government has conducted more military actions against its neighbors than any other major country in the world."

Indeed, I suspect few Americans appreciate just how often the Chinese Communist Party has attacked its neighbors. This bloody history, along with the party's recent actions and words, tells the same story: China is preparing for war.

The Bloody History of Chinese Communist Aggression

Far from exhausted after two decades of civil war, the victorious Chinese Communist Party immediately turned outward, attacking, invading, or sowing revolution. By any measure, Communist China was one of the most aggressive countries of the twentieth century.

Barely a year after winning the Chinese Civil War, Mao Zedong intervened in the Korean War to save his fellow Communists. While our troops supported the South Korean government, Chinese soldiers flooded into

Communist North Korea, attacking our forces and contributing to more than 36,000 American deaths during the war. Our troops gave as good as they got and then some, killing an estimated 400,000 Chinese combatants, including Mao's eldest son, who served as a liaison with Soviet troops. The Korean War ended only after Dwight Eisenhower became president and hinted at using nuclear weapons to settle the conflict.

During the war, the United States also stationed our Navy's Seventh Fleet between Mao and his archenemy, Chiang Kai-shek, the former president of China who was deposed by Mao and who had fled to Taiwan. Chiang used the breathing room to build Taiwan, about one hundred miles off the Chinese coast, into an anti-Communist fortress while fortifying several smaller islands closer to the mainland.

But an undeterred Mao launched an attack on Taiwan within a year of the end of the Korean War. In what has become known as the First Taiwan Strait Crisis, Mao shelled and seized several of Chiang's smaller islands near the mainland. The crisis ended when Congress authorized President Eisenhower to use any means necessary to defend Taiwan.

Three years later, Mao said he wanted to "probe the attitude of the Americans in Washington," so he attacked Taiwan again to seize some of these smaller outlying islands; Communist forces bombarded one island with nearly a half million artillery shells. In response, Eisenhower deployed a naval armada, armed with tactical nuclear weapons, to defend the islands. Faced again with the threat of superior American power, Mao ended the main hostilities. Yet China continued to shell some of Taiwan's smaller islands—on odd-numbered days, bizarrely—for more than twenty years, a practice that continued after Mao's death and until Jimmy Carter diplomatically recognized the Communist regime in 1979.

To its south, China also has repeatedly attacked India. With the United States distracted in 1962 during the Cuban Missile Crisis, Mao launched a sneak attack against India in the Himalayan Mountains. Eighty thousand Chinese Communists invaded, killed more than eight thousand Indians, and seized fifteen thousand square miles of Indian territory. Mao concluded this opportunistic war shortly after the Cuban Missile Crisis ended and before the United States could intervene. Five years later, he again attacked India, killing hundreds. This time, however, he faced a more prepared adversary, and India repulsed the Communist assault.

China spread yet more mayhem in Southeast Asia. Mao backed a Communist insurgency led by the bloodthirsty revolutionary Ho Chi Minh aimed at toppling French colonial rule in Indochina after World War II. The insurgency succeeded and splintered the region into North Vietnam, South Vietnam, Laos, and Cambodia. Chinese meddling then devastated each country in the years ahead.

In the ensuing struggle for a Communist takeover of all Southeast Asia, Mao first armed Communist North Vietnam in its war against South Vietnam. Between 1956 and 1963, China supplied North Vietnam with an estimated 10,000 artillery pieces, 270,000 guns, 2 million artillery shells, 200 million bullets, and dozens of ships and planes. Mao increased aid further once our troops arrived in South Vietnam: China supplied an estimated 30 percent of North Vietnam's military needs and sent hundreds of thousands of soldiers to prop up North Vietnam. Meanwhile, Mao also supported the Pathet Lao, a Communist insurgency in Laos, and aided in the construction of the infamous Ho Chi Minh Trail through eastern Laos, which China and North Vietnam used to arm the Communist Vietcong guerrillas in South Vietnam. By the end, China had contributed to the deaths of 58,000 Americans and millions of Vietnamese and Laotian civilians. And Mao lived to see both South Vietnam and Laos fall to his fellow Communists in 1975.

Mao also lived to see his protégé, the genocidal maniac Pol Pot, seize power in Cambodia. Mao inspired, funded, armed, trained, clothed, and fed the Khmer Rouge, Pol Pot's radical Communist movement. Pol Pot abolished money, closed markets, collectivized farms, banned religion, and forcibly emptied Cambodia's cities. In his infamous "killing fields," he murdered an estimated 1.7 million people—nearly a quarter of the Cambodian population.

As with thieves, though, there's no honor among Communists. China and Vietnam have an ancient history of tensions, and as communism swept the region, these tensions resurfaced. Vietnam insulted China by tending to side with Soviet Russia during Communist infighting. In 1974, China seized all South Vietnam's positions in the strategically valuable Paracel Islands, which North Vietnam had planned to take for itself. Worse, Mao refused to return the Paracels when North Vietnam overran South Vietnam. A few years later, Vietnam invaded Cambodia with Soviet support and toppled the Chinese Communist–backed Pol Pot. China responded by invading Vietnam, with Deng Xiaoping taunting that China would "teach Vietnam a lesson." In fact, the outnumbered but battle-hardened Vietnamese taught China a lesson, killing at least thirty thousand Chinese soldiers in two months—more deaths than the United States suffered in its deadliest two years in Vietnam.

While Mao fomented terror to the southeast, trouble was also brewing with Soviet Russia to the north. Between 1964 and 1969, China and Russia had four thousand incidents along their border. In early 1969, Chinese forces ambushed Russian forces over a remote river island on the two countries' Siberian border; the intense exchange of fire resulted in hundreds of casualties between the two sides. By October 1969, relations had deteriorated so badly that Mao left Beijing, fearing that the Russians might launch a nuclear attack.

Beyond invading and terrorizing its neighbors, Chinese Communists also sowed civil war, repression, and chaos around the world. In *Maoism: A Global History,* Julia Lovell describes how China supported or inspired bloody civil wars in Malaysia, Indonesia, India, Nepal, and Peru, while also championing a dizzying array of Communist regimes and revolutionaries, from Palestinian terrorists to Algerian insurgents.

After decades of war on nearly every front, the Chinese Communists adopted a more cautious approach, one focused on the long term. Deng Xiaoping famously instructed his party to "hide your strength, bide your time." In the following decades, Chinese diplomats feigned benign passivity, allowing the party to build trust with the West and lull it into complacency.

The only notable exception to the hide-and-bide strategy was Taiwan. Time and again, Chinese leaders snarled to their Western counterparts that the island is a breakaway province and must be united with the mainland, by force if necessary. But American leaders consistently defended Taiwan's autonomy and refused to allow the Chinese Communists to conquer the strategically vital island. The issue came to a head during Taiwan's 1996 elections, when China tried to intimidate the island into electing a pro-Beijing president. In what became known as the Third Taiwan Strait Crisis, China mobilized one hundred thousand soldiers and fired missiles into waters barely twenty miles off Taiwan's coast. Beijing even alluded to the use of nuclear weapons against America. President Bill Clinton responded by dispatching two aircraft-carrier battle groups to the vicinity of Taiwan—a show of strength that China couldn't match. China backed down, the election proceeded as planned, and the Taiwanese people reelected their anti-Beijing and pro-democracy president.

China bitterly swallowed the humiliation of the Third Taiwan Strait Crisis and resumed its hide-and-bide strategy with America. But behind its compliant demeanor, the Communist Party began a military buildup to ensure it never suffered such humiliation again.

A One-Sided Arms Race

Over the last quarter century, the Chinese Communist Party has undertaken one of the biggest military build-ups in history. The People's Liberation Army is both the military wing of the party and the nation's armed forces—in that order. The party has increased military spending for the PLA by more than 1,000 percent, building a military more sophisticated than Soviet Russia's ever was and comparable in size to Nazi Germany's before World War II. The party's four-million-man military is the largest in the world, around twice the size of our military and nearly as technologically advanced. This massive investment of national resources speaks volumes about the party's intentions.

The PLA is the largest ground force in the world—970,000 soldiers strong. By contrast, the U.S. Army has shrunk to its smallest size since the start of World War II, with barely 470,000 active-duty soldiers. The party uses the PLA most often as the tool of last resort to restore domestic order, as at the Tiananmen Square Massacre in 1989. But it remains a potent adversary, as we've seen, to China's neighbors.

The party has also rapidly expanded its maritime forces, building the world's largest navy, coast guard, and maritime militia, along with the largest commercial fishing fleet, which can be weaponized if needed. Our Navy, on the other hand, has shrunk to its smallest size since World War I. And the gap will only grow. A single Chinese shipyard can produce more vessels than all America's shipyards combined—and China has thirteen shipyards. The PLA Navy, like ours, also includes a marine corps—and it has tripled in size, with plans to reach one hundred thousand marines.

China similarly has transformed its air forces. In 2000, two-thirds of China's fighter aircraft were junky relics from the 1950s. Today, the PLA has the world's third largest and second most advanced air force. Again, the contrast with the U.S. Air Force is alarming: our fleet has never been smaller, older, or less ready for combat. The PLA's planes are on average newer, similar in quality, equipped with nearly equivalent radars, and armed with longer-range, bigger, and faster missiles. To put it bluntly, a Chinese pilot will see his American adversary at the same time, but will be able to fire a missile and escape before the American pilot can lock on with his own missile.

The Communist Party has invested above all in "area denial" weapons designed to keep American forces away from Taiwan and the Chinese mainland. This arsenal includes the world's largest submarine fleet, biggest stock of sea mines, and first-ever anti-ship ballistic missiles. And those missiles are just part of the world's largest ballistic-missile stockpile, with at least five hundred missiles capable of striking targets 3,400 miles away—putting America's military base on Guam comfortably in range. Xi Jinping prioritizes these long-range missiles so highly that he elevated the PLA's Rocket Force to its own branch of the military, on par with the army, navy, and air force.

China also commands several advanced, unconventional military tools such as cyber, drone, satellite, and anti-satellite technologies. Chinese hackers have methodically targeted our water, power, and transportation infrastructure to sow chaos in the American homeland in the event of war. A single Chinese company manufactures more than 70 percent of the world's drones, enabling China to pioneer offensive "drone swarm" tactics or to maximize tactical surveillance on the battlefield. The party nearly doubled the number of intelligence satellites in orbit between 2018 and 2022, leaving it second only to America, while also investing in anti-satellite weapons designed to blind U.S. forces.

To be sure, the United States retains advantages against China. The PLA can build and train for war, but that's different from actually fighting a war, which the PLA hasn't done since Vietnam embarrassed it in 1979. As I sometimes heard in the Army, "when the ramp drops, the bullshit stops." You can train all you want, but until the ramp drops on, say, an infantry fighting vehicle or a C-130 cargo plane and your troops get into the fight, you can't know for sure how they'll perform. This maxim would apply especially should the PLA attempt to invade Taiwan, which would be one of the most complicated military operations in history. Similarly, the United States has a broad network of allies and partners for a potential conflict with China, none of whom want to be a Chinese vassal state. And even if the PLA outpaces our military in raw numbers, we retain the technological edge.

But still. As Stalin reputedly said, quantity has a quality all its own, and the PLA has a quantitative military advantage unrivaled in the world, while steadily closing the qualitative gap. Mao famously said that "power comes out of the barrel of a gun." His disciples now have more guns than anyone else. What's more, China is now amassing the most dangerous weapons of all: a vast nuclear arsenal.

A "Breathtaking" Nuclear Arsenal

Under Xi Jinping, the Chinese Communist Party is building more nuclear weapons faster than it ever has. China's nuclear forces not only threaten our national survival and way of life, but also embolden the Communist Party by providing a nuclear umbrella for its huge conventional military.

During the Cold War, Mao, the father of China's nuclear program, was possibly the most nonchalant leader about nuclear war. A nuclear apocalypse, in his judgment, could hasten global Communist revolution: "If the worst came to the worst and half of mankind died, the other half would remain while imperialism would be razed to the ground and the whole world would become socialist." Unsurprisingly for a genocidal mass murderer, he shrugged at the prospect of unthinkable deaths among his own people: "What if they killed three hundred million of us? We would still have many people left." When China detonated its first nuclear weapon in 1964, a giddy Mao celebrated with a bizarre missive, "Atom bomb goes off when it is told. Ah, what boundless joy!" One can only assume it's more poetic in the original Chinese.

After Mao's death, Deng Xiaoping applied the hide-and-bide strategy to nuclear weapons. He placated rivals by referring to China's nuclear weapons as "just symbolic" and by embracing a policy of "minimum deterrence" by which China would build only enough nuclear weapons to deter an attack, not enough to launch a first strike. As a result, China had what's known as a no-first-use policy. Aside from during the Third Taiwan Strait Crisis, the party generally avoided nuclear saber rattling. Deng's hide-and-bide nuclear strategy also allowed China to avoid international pressure to sign arms-control treaties.

But Xi scrapped the minimalist hide-and-bide nuclear strategy as soon as he took power, insisting that the party's nuclear weapons were a "pillar of our status as a great power." Since then, China's nuclear arsenal has grown at "breathtaking" rates, as the last two commanders of U.S. nuclear forces have testified to one of my Senate committees. China had 240 nuclear warheads when Xi became the paramount leader. Just ten years on, Xi had more than doubled that number to over 500 warheads. By the end of this decade, China plans to double it again to more than 1,000 warheads. The Pentagon estimates that China will have stockpiled 1,500 nuclear warheads—an astonishing 525 percent increase since Xi took power—by 2035, though given the Pentagon's consistent underestimates in the past, it's fair (and safer) to assume that China will move even faster.

China's path to 1,500 nuclear warheads also serves as a reminder that China isn't bound by any nuclear arms-control treaty, unlike the United States. Fifteen hundred warheads are almost as many strategic nuclear weapons as the United States and Russia can deploy by treaty. (Both nations have more warheads in storage.) Thus, China could achieve nuclear parity in a decade at most—and probably faster—and then continue to deploy nuclear weapons unconstrained by treaty obligations.

Put bluntly, while we have nuclear superiority over China for now, the day is fast approaching when China's nuclear forces will overmatch ours. And given what Xi has called his "no-limits" partnership with Russia, those two nations combined already overmatch America's nuclear forces today.

Yet it's not only the quantity of China's nuclear weapons that should concern us, but also the quality. Like America, China fields a nuclear "triad": land-based missiles, submarine-launched missiles, and bomber aircraft. Unlike our aging triad, though, China's triad is much newer and more advanced. For example, China has built more than three hundred new silos for brand-new missiles in recent years. China is also developing dangerous new delivery systems outside the classic triad. In 2021, for instance, the PLA successfully tested a hypersonic missile capable of delivering a nuclear warhead. These missiles travel at several times the speed of sound from any direction, evading our Arctic-based early-warning radar.

Not surprisingly given this all-out nuclear buildup, our senior military leaders believe that China is abandoning its long-standing no-first-use policy. So do I. Why else invest so much money and effort in its nuclear forces?

And it's no coincidence that China is racing to expand its nuclear arsenal exactly when it has turned outward.

Rising Chinese Aggression

With its growing military strength, the Communist Party has returned to Mao's aggressive ways. China is pressing vast territorial claims on its borders, while testing the United States around the world. The Communists are no longer biding their time or hiding their strength because they think their time has come.

After the Great Recession of 2008, the party saw its opportunity to challenge a distracted West; 2009 became widely known as China's "year of assertiveness." In 2009 alone, China lashed out economically and diplomatically against the Philippines, Japan, South Korea, Australia, Norway, and Denmark. Chinese aircraft and ships surrounded and harassed an unarmed U.S. Navy ship in the South China Sea. The party embarrassed Barack Obama on his first visit to China as president, lecturing him, arresting dissidents, and strictly controlling his schedule. Secretary of State Hillary Clinton later recalled that "hide and bide" was turning into "show and tell."

Xi Jinping continued this aggressive turn with breathtaking power grabs. Barely a year into power, he asserted Chinese control over two-thirds of the airspace in the East China Sea, illegitimately demanding that foreign aircraft follow Beijing's edicts and air-traffic-control instructions. This zone intrudes suspiciously close to our military base in Okinawa and cuts deeply into Japanese airspace. As a result, Japan scrambled its military jets against Chinese aircraft 575 times in 2022—versus fewer than 50 times in 2009.

Xi also asserts effective dominion over most of the East China Sea itself. The sea is rich with natural resources and islands of strategic value, especially Japan's Senkaku Islands. Xi has expanded his predecessor's practice of sending Chinese vessels through the islands' territorial waters to use the Chinese Coast Guard to assert law-enforcement control over the islands in a slow-motion maritime invasion. In 2022, China's coast guard spent more than three hundred days in these waters. These aggressive incursions aren't a small, remote nuisance; rather, they threaten to provoke a war with the United States. We have a defense treaty with Japan, and it covers the Senkaku Islands, which the secretary of defense reaffirmed in 2023.

Even more astonishing are China's claims to 90 percent of the South China Sea. This massive sea is more than twice the size of Alaska, carries more than one-fifth of the world's commerce, and contains more oil and gas reserves than all of Europe. China's preposterous claims extend into the territorial waters of the Philippines, Malaysia, Vietnam, and other nations. An international maritime tribunal repudiated these claims in 2016, yet China still asserts them with its naval power and its outposts in the Paracel Islands—which Mao seized in 1974—and the Spratly Islands.

Perhaps more than anything, these artificial islands reveal China's methods and ambitions. In many cases, these "islands" are little more than atolls, rocky outcroppings, or sand bars at low tide. While other nations have asserted their claims in the South China Sea by improving these features, nothing compares to what China has done. Early in Xi's tenure, China dredged and reclaimed seventeen times more land in just twenty months than all other countries combined over the previous forty years. Thus far, Xi has created 3,200 acres of new islands in the South China Sea. What's worse, China has militarized these islands despite Xi's public promise to Obama not to do so. What were once uninhabitable sandy shoals with a few small bushes are now military bases with huge runways, aircraft hangars, missile batteries, munition bunkers, radar sites, barracks, and even swimming pools.

The strategic significance of these militarized artificial islands cannot be overstated. The island bases not only strengthen China's maritime claims, but also extend the range of the PLA's fighters, bombers, and missiles by hundreds of miles. China uses the islands to surveil activity across the South China Sea and could use them to control one of the world's most critical waterways, threatening the U.S. Navy and economic trade.

And Xi sees the advantage he has gained. China regularly threatens our Navy for sailing in the vicinity of these islands. Xi personally warned the Philippine president over a dispute in the Spratlys, "We don't want to quarrel with you, but if you force the issue, we'll go to war." As with Japan, we're treaty-bound to aid the Philippines against a Chinese attack.

Xi is up to the same tricks on land, too, as India learned in 2020, when Chinese forces brutally attacked Indian soldiers in the Himalayas, killing at least twenty. In a nighttime assault, Chinese troops threw Indians over cliffs, slit their throats, or clubbed them to death. It was the deadliest Himalayan border clash in more than fifty years. Xi rationalized the unprovoked attack as Mao often had, by asserting to the U.S. secretary of defense that "we cannot lose even one inch of territory left behind by our ancestors." This sweeping assertion, of course, could justify Chinese aggression against most of its neighbors.

Meanwhile, China has begun to organize a powerful anti-American alliance. As we've seen, Xi forged a "no-limits" partnership with Russia, the world's largest nuclear power. He has also strengthened China's relationship with Iran, the world's worst state sponsor of terrorism, while continuing China's longtime support for North Korea's outlaw regime. Of late, Xi is making inroads in our backyard. In 2023, Cuba's Communist dictator proclaimed that relations with China were at an "all-time high" and agreed to host a Chinese spy base barely one hundred miles from our shores. China also deepened its relationship with Venezuela to an "all-weather" strategic partnership.

China wants to use this rogue's gallery of rogue states to strain U.S. alliances and stretch our resources. For instance, Russia's war on Ukraine and Iran's terror campaign against Israel forced the United States to commit significant resources in two separate regions, while China masses its forces in the Western Pacific.

And China is also extending outward by building overseas military bases. In 2017, China opened its first overseas base in the African nation of Djibouti, just a few miles from America's only permanent base on the continent. China also built a naval base in Cambodia to press further its advantages in the South China Sea. The Pentagon estimates that China is exploring military bases in at least eighteen other countries, including on Africa's western coast, to have a clear shot at our Navy in the Atlantic.

Nor does China shy from flexing its muscles within America itself. In 2023, China brazenly floated a spy balloon across the continental United States and sent warships into our sovereign waters off Alaska. China also routinely targets America for cyberattacks, more than does any other nation.

But nowhere is the Chinese threat more acute than on the island of Taiwan.

The Next Taiwan Strait Crisis

Taiwan is the most dangerous flashpoint in the world. In three separate Taiwan Strait crises, the Chinese Communist Party went to the brink over Taiwan until the United States backed it down. But after decades of military preparation and renewed Communist aggression, China is unlikely to back down again. And the stakes couldn't be higher.

The Chinese Communist Party has claimed and coveted Taiwan from the beginning. Imperial China ruled Taiwan for centuries before losing the island in 1895 to Japan, which lost it back to Chinese control after World War II. When the Communists won the Chinese Civil War in 1949, the Nationalist government of China escaped the mainland to Taiwan. Ever since, the Communist Party has viewed Taiwan as unsettled business.

But it's not just old grievances: Taiwan is key strategic terrain in the Western Pacific. The island, about one hundred miles off the Chinese coast, sits between the East and South China Seas and belongs to the "first island chain," along with Japan and the Philippines. This island chain of pro-American democracies with a large American military presence hems in China and thwarts its ability to project power beyond its shores. Taiwan is the linchpin of the island chain; General Douglas MacArthur famously called the island "an unsinkable aircraft carrier and submarine tender." Without Taiwan, China can't achieve its ambitions for global dominance.

Chinese Communists have always understood this geographic reality and have tried to intimidate us from supporting Taiwan. When President-elect Donald Trump accepted a congratulatory call from Taiwan's president in December 2016, China's foreign minister condemned the "petty trick." I told President-elect Trump that it was the right decision to demonstrate his support for the peaceful status quo. House Speaker Nancy Pelosi's trip to Taiwan in August 2022 further enraged the Communists. They called it "a serious provocation" and threatened that China "will not allow any foreign force to bully, suppress, or enslave us." I bumped into Speaker Pelosi shortly before her trip and encouraged her; she lamented that Biden White House officials had leaked the news to pressure her not to go. At a 2023 meeting with Biden, Xi reportedly "stressed that the Taiwan question is at the very core of China's core interests" and was the "biggest, most potentially dangerous issue." In a New Year's address a few weeks later, Xi declared that "the reunification of the motherland is a historical inevitability."

More worrisome than rhetoric, of course, are China's growing military threats against Taiwan. China's massive military buildup is designed above all to blockade and invade Taiwan. In the meantime, the PLA regularly rehearses the operation, which probes and strains Taiwan's defenses, while also reducing warning time for a future invasion. In 2020, for instance, China staged its most aggressive exercises since the Third Taiwan Strait

Crisis, infringing on Taiwan's airspace and waters and practicing military strikes on mock U.S. aircraft carriers. In 2022, Chinese aircraft flew into Taiwan's airspace more than 1,700 times, more than the previous three years combined. China's military response to Pelosi's trip was especially aggressive: it encircled Taiwan with aircraft and ships and conducted live-fire exercises with artillery and missiles, some of which landed in Japanese waters. And China matched the incursions into Taiwan's airspace in 2023, showing no desire to reduce tensions.

Yet the United States and Taiwan remain unprepared for the coming storm. As we've seen, the military balance of power is shifting rapidly in China's favor. The United States will soon be historically weak at sea and is also losing its competitive edge in the air. Perhaps worse, our military has only enough munitions to last a week or two in a war with China over Taiwan. Nor can our defense industry manufacture enough weapons to solve this "empty bins" problem anytime soon.

Taiwan's defenses are in worse shape. Despite the singular threat, Taiwan spends only 2.6 percent of its economy on defense. In their alarming *Danger Zone: The Coming Conflict with China*, Michael Beckley and Hal Brands warn that China outspends Taiwan by a factor of twenty-five to one on defense, most Taiwanese tanks and attack helicopters are dysfunctional, and Taiwan has slashed its active-duty military by a hundred thousand troops.

As a senator, I regularly review war games between

China and the United States—exercises where military experts play out what would happen in a war between the two nations. I've never seen happy results. While some war games are classified and others not, there's no secret about the depressing outcomes. China often wins. After one such war game, the vice chairman of the Joint Chiefs of Staff said that the American strategy "failed miserably" and that the Chinese "just ran rings around us." A 2023 war game by the House Select Committee on the Chinese Communist Party similarly found that China would succeed in landing eighty thousand soldiers on Taiwan, despite U.S. resistance.

Even when China fails, the war games end with unspeakably high costs. In one war game, conducted by the Center for Strategic and International Studies, the United States prevailed but lost nearly three hundred planes and seventeen ships, including two aircraft carriers. These would be the worst loss of aircraft since the Vietnam War and worst naval losses since World War II. The United States also suffered nearly ten thousand casualties—almost half the total casualties we took in the entire wars in Afghanistan and Iraq.

Though Taiwan may seem like a small, remote island, the stakes couldn't be higher. What General MacArthur said three-quarters of a century ago remains true today: "The domination of [Taiwan] by an unfriendly power would be a disaster of utmost importance to the United States." The Chinese Communists covet Taiwan not merely to right a perceived, but parochial, historical wrong; they know that control of Taiwan would put China on the path to global dominance over the United States. And not just military dominance, but also economic supremacy. I'll explain the natural and logical consequences of a successful Chinese invasion of Taiwan in chapter 7, "China Could Win," but suffice it to say for now that, in short order, China would call the global shots and America's way of life would be poorer, more anxious, and more dangerous.

Maybe this scenario seems farfetched. After all, not since the War of 1812 against Great Britain has the United States faced an economically superior enemy. Some might doubt that China would inflict such grave harm on its biggest export market. But there's little reason for doubt. And while it may be unpopular to say in some quarters, I have to say it: Even without Taiwan, China has exploited America's workers and businesses on its way to becoming the world's second largest economy. That economic growth, in turn, has fueled China's military buildup. The United States foolishly abetted China's rise, in effect paying for many of those Chinese missiles, ships, aircraft, and nuclear weapons. If we want to see what China would do after a war for Taiwan, the best place to look is at what it's already done for the last four decades.

III.

IIIIIIIIIIIIIIIIIIIIIIIIIIIIIIIIIII

China Is Waging
Economic World War

In 2018, President Donald Trump retaliated against Chinese intellectual-property theft by imposing a tax on certain Chinese imports. A CNBC headline screamed, "Trade War Begins." The *New York Times* concurred, writing that "a trade war between the world's two largest economies officially began" with Trump's decision. The *Washington Post* branded it the "Trump Trade War."

Yet Trump didn't start a trade war in 2018. China did, nearly two decades earlier. In 2000, the United States granted China permanent most-favored-nation status, which provided China with generous trading terms. This concession enabled China to join the World Trade Organization the next year—after which China promptly launched an economic world war.

The Chinese Communist Party's economic strategy can be summed up in three words: "lie, cheat, and steal." China has stolen trillions of dollars of wealth, crippled entire industries, seized control of developing technologies, destroyed millions of American jobs, and extorted entire countries with its newfound economic power.

Since 2001, China's economy has grown more than 1,200 percent—equal to $16 trillion—the spoils of perhaps the most successful and one-sided economic contest in history. And the losers are America and you, in the form of fewer jobs, lower wages, shoddier products, and a more dangerous world.

Rigging the Game

Xi Jinping once lectured the elites at the World Economic Forum in Davos, Switzerland, that "we should commit ourselves to growing an open global economy," but he and his party have ruthlessly exploited that openness. The Chinese Communist Party has manipulated China's currency, created state-backed corporate giants, illegally dumped subsidized products into foreign markets, enslaved its people, and destroyed its environment. China didn't win a global economic competition; it rigged the game.

When the Western world welcomed China into the World Trade Organization, the Chinese Communists' promises proved no more genuine than their commitments to Tibet or Hong Kong. China promised to open its economy, compete fairly, and play by international rules—supposedly creating a market of 1.4 billion customers for American businesses. Western leaders believed that the ties of commerce would promote peaceful growth and friendly relations with China, while also bringing freedom to the Chinese people. Instead, with our leaders busy waging a global "war on terror" after the September 11 attacks, China's leaders started their global economic conquest, recalling the famous quote often attributed to Vladimir Lenin: "The capitalists will sell us the rope with which we will hang them."

As with all things in China, the Chinese Communist Party—not market forces—exercises total control over China's currency. China almost immediately began devaluing its currency, which made Chinese goods cheaper to sell to Americans and thus gave its manufacturers an illegal advantage over American workers and businesses. Currency manipulation helped China more even than did its low wages: in *China After Mao: The Rise of a Superpower*, Frank Dikötter writes that "since the yuan was undervalued by somewhere between 15 to 25 per cent, not even Bangladesh was able to compete, even though its wages were 20 to 30 per cent lower than those in China." In 2014, the Economic Policy Institute estimated that currency manipulation contributed up to $900 billion a year to global trade deficits, with China the worst offender. China continued to manipulate its currency for years; the U.S. Treasury Department designated it a currency manipulator as late as 2019. These years of currency manipulation contributed to our nation's total trade deficit of more than $6 trillion with China since 2001.

The Chinese Communist Party not only manipulated China's currency, but also directly controls up to 40 percent of China's economy through 150,000 government-owned companies. In 1997, Jiang Zemin directed the party to "grasp the big and let go of the small" in the economy. In other words, the party wouldn't bother with small nonstrategic businesses but would control and support the largest, most important industries. As a result, by 2022 nearly one in five Fortune Global 500 companies were Chinese government–owned enterprises.

China's government-backed industries now produce more cement, steel, and ships than the rest of the world combined. The party's corporate behemoths also process nearly 90 percent of the world's rare-earth elements, which are essential to manufacturing everything electronic, from your smartphone to your computer to your car.

These companies achieved their dominant positions because foreign companies weren't competing with Chinese businesses; they were battling the Chinese state. These Chinese companies could sell products at cost or even at a loss because, unlike foreign competitors, they had a government backstop. Private businesses were simply no match. No corporation, no matter its size, could rival the power of the Chinese Communist Party—especially when our government too often left American businesses and workers to fight alone against these impossible odds.

China also provides more subsidies and artificial support to its businesses than does any other nation. The Center for Strategic and International Studies found the state spent the equivalent of $407 billion supporting Chinese industry in 2019 alone, up from $390 billion in 2018 and $375 billion in 2017. China provides everything from direct monetary subsidies to tax credits to reduced rent. By comparison, the United States spent less than $85 billion in 2019 to support our industries. To take one specific example, Congress dedicated nearly $53 billion in 2022 to support domestic semiconductor manufacturing, but China unveiled its own plan that year to inject an additional $143 billion into the Chinese semiconductor industry, bringing the total to $322 billion.

American and other Western businesses aren't just competing against Beijing-backed companies, either; they're battling a hydra of provincial and local Chinese governments. These governments operate two-thirds of China's state-owned enterprises. In a cutthroat competition with one another known as "the mayor economy," local officials cut checks, sell land at bargain basement prices, and turn a blind eye to virtually any corporate abuse—all benefiting Chinese companies over foreign companies. And because many Chinese cities have more people than midsize European nations, these Communist chieftains command resources comparable to those commanded by heads of state.

China also condemns millions of its subjects to modern-day slavery, forcing them to work in sweltering cotton fields, miserable factories, and on dangerous fishing trawlers. What's more, the Communists' "hukou" system, a kind of household-registration system—and, really, a de facto caste system—denies social services to hundreds of millions of rural Chinese workers and thus forces them into low-paying big-city jobs. These abhorrent methods artificially lower wages and give Chinese companies yet another edge over foreign competitors. After all, how can textile workers in South Carolina compete against slaves or indentured servants in Xinjiang or Tibet? They can't, because their wages will always be higher and their hours fewer.

As with other dictatorial regimes, Chinese Communists have allowed companies to destroy their environment to keep costs low. Up to 90 percent of China's groundwater and around half its river water are now undrinkable. Farmers can't even use much of the nation's fresh water for their crops, fearing it might either kill the plant or poison the person who eats it. In addition, more than a million Chinese die each year from outdoor air pollution, with state-backed factories spewing soot, heavy metals, and toxins into the air. The price for decades of deliberate indifference to public health is high, but the party is happy to let the Chinese people pay instead of its state-backed businesses.

Put simply, China has spent trillions of dollars in subsidies, weaponized its currency, and abused and poisoned its people to stack the economic deck against foreign competitors. But that's only the half of it; the party has also extorted and robbed that foreign competition as well.

Gangster Economics

The Chinese Communist Party operates in the global economy like a gangster in a world without police. China steals foreign technology and shakes down foreign companies on an unprecedented scale. The FBI director has rightly called China's gangster tactics "one of the largest transfers of wealth in human history."

According to the bipartisan Intellectual Property Commission, the United States loses between $225 and $600 billion from intellectual-property theft *every single year.* Some of the most valuable assets in the modern economy—patents, trade secrets, blueprints, sensitive data, formulas, and so forth—are at risk. And China is by far the most prolific thief. In 2019, one in five North American companies reported that China had stolen their intellectual property in the previous year. As of 2021, the Department of Justice linked the Chinese state to 80 percent of all economic espionage cases. In a comic twist, our own ports reflect the vast scale of the Communist theft: between 60 and 75 percent of the counterfeit and pirated goods seized at the ports originate from Chinese thieves.

China engages in unprecedented cyber warfare to pursue these ill-gotten gains. In one recent example, a single Chinese cyber campaign—dubbed Operation CuckooBees in 2022—reportedly pilfered trillions of dollars' worth of intellectual property from thirty multinational companies. The hackers apparently targeted secrets critical to advanced industries identified in Made in China 2025, the party's scheme to seize the "commanding heights" of the international economy. In an earlier instance, called Operation Aurora, Chinese hackers targeted more than two dozen American companies, including Dow Chemical, Morgan Stanley, and Google. In yet another sign of China's gangster methods, only Google—which is already severely restricted in China—named Chinese hackers as the culprits; the rest feared retaliation.

But China also uses old-fashioned espionage—spies by the thousands, to be exact. Hundreds of thousands of Chinese students and researchers are usually present in America. No doubt many Chinese nationals come here to work productively, study diligently, and experience freedom, often for the first time. But among this army of visitors are battalions of party agents, conspiring to rob the companies, universities, and labs that generously welcomed them.

The examples of economic espionage are legion. In 2015, a Chinese researcher stole DNA samples and research from a Yale geneticist to enable China's police state to target the Uyghur people. In 2019, two Chinese researchers at Harvard tried to steal twenty-one vials of biological research on cancer cells. Between 2006 and 2010, a Chinese student at Duke University allegedly stole research from his American mentor's lab and then founded a multibillion-dollar company and branded himself "China's Elon Musk." Worse still, the stolen research related to so-called quantum invisibility, a technology designed to make an object—say, a fighter jet—invisible to radar. No one with good sense can explain why a Chinese national was allowed to work on a project with an obvious and critical military application.

America's biggest and most sophisticated companies aren't exempt. In 2017, a Chinese engineer at Coca-Cola stole over $100 million worth of trade secrets and then opened a multibillion-dollar company in China with government funding. In 2018, an Apple employee abruptly quit his job and tried to flee to China with trade secrets related to the company's self-driving car technology. In 2024, the Department of Justice arrested a former Google engineer for stealing hundreds of files related to artificial intelligence while also serving as CEO of a Chinese company.

Nor is my own state exempt. Chinese researchers working at a government-funded rice research center in Stuttgart, Arkansas, and in Kansas stole millions of dollars' worth of proprietary rice-seed technology and handed it over to a Chinese crop institute. And I still remember the call I got from the FBI in 2020 to inform me of imminent charges against a University of Arkansas professor related to research conducted in part for NASA and the U.S. Air Force.

The Chinese Communists are even more antagonistic against foreign companies operating within China's borders. China routinely forces foreign companies into joint ventures with Chinese companies as a condition of doing business there. Next, the party orders the foreign companies to transfer key technology to their Chinese partner. The DuPont Corporation surrendered proprietary chemical technology; General Electric turned over cutting-edge airplane electronics; General Motors transferred sophisticated electric-vehicle technology; and IBM handed over partial blueprints to its high-end servers and the software running them—all simply to access the Chinese market.

Yet even these joint ventures don't buy protection from Chinese theft. For instance, a Chinese employee of General Electric stole turbine technologies from the company in 2018. The case of DuPont is worse, but typical. DuPont suspended its relationship with its Chinese partner in 2013 over suspected theft of intellectual property. Four years later, DuPont believed that its former partner was still ripping it off and entered arbitration.

In response, China's antitrust enforcer dispatched twenty officers to raid DuPont's Shanghai offices to retaliate against DuPont and intimidate the company into silence.

Put simply, foreign companies are living on borrowed time in China, in no small part because the Chinese Communist Party actively conspires with Chinese companies in these economic crimes. For example, Chinese law deters foreign companies from protecting their intellectual property by threatening them with million-dollar weekly fines if they sue anywhere but in the corrupt Chinese courts. China welcomes foreign companies only until it can stand up Chinese competitors, then the party will marginalize or drive out the foreigners. Xi may talk at Davos about an "open global economy," but the party doesn't want to partner with foreign companies; it wants to replace them. China wants a Baidu for every Google and an Alibaba for every Amazon—and then it wants to destroy the foreign competition.

Once China dominates its home market, it invades foreign markets. Remember this the next time you see an ad for Shein or TikTok—or the next time a politician advocates for more green energy.

Green Is the New Red

There's perhaps no better example of the Chinese Communist Party's rigged game and gangster tactics than so-called green energy. Using the methods we've seen, China has cornered the global market on solar power, wind energy, and electric vehicles. Many Western politicians champion green energy under the banner of climate change, but it looks an awful lot like the red five-star flag of the People's Republic of China.

China took over global solar manufacturing by using the party's entire kit of unfair trade practices. In 2000, China produced barely 1 percent of the world's solar cells; by 2023, it controlled 80 percent of the market. China now dominates every stage of the manufacturing process, and if the trend continues, it will soon control 95 percent of the global market.

In *No Trade Is Free*, former U.S. trade representative Robert Lighthizer explains that "the regime pulled out all the stops—massive subsidies flowed from the central and provincial governments, a depreciated currency boosted competitiveness, provincial governments subsidized land and electricity, state-backed banks offered cheap financing, and government contracts went exclusively to Chinese firms." All told, China has invested hundreds of billions of dollars to seize control of global solar manufacturing—and that doesn't count the Uyghur slave labor that Chinese solar companies use to cut costs.

As a result, China has devastated yet another American industry. Unsurprisingly, Chinese solar panels sold for much less than American alternatives; between 2012 and 2016, American imports of Chinese solar panels surged

500 percent. Only ten American solar manufacturers remained when Donald Trump imposed hefty tariffs on Chinese solar imports.

China then tried to evade the tariffs by routing its solar panels through Southeast Asian countries. President Biden's own Commerce Department acted to block these trans-shipped imports, but he intervened to waive the penalties. My fellow senators and I introduced legislation to reverse President Biden's decision, and the bill passed with bipartisan majorities. While I have my doubts about the potential of solar power, I certainly don't want American workers and businesses harmed by China yet again. Unfortunately, President Biden vetoed the bill. When it comes to China's predatory trade practices, some politicians never learn.

China used the same tricks to become the world's dominant wind-energy manufacturer, supplying the turbines for 60 percent of new wind power in 2022. The party forced a Spanish company to turn over cutting-edge wind technology and stole computer technology from an American company. The Chinese government doesn't subsidize merely its wind companies; it also subsidizes everything from the steel in the turbines to the coal for the steel mill to the shipyards that build the ships to install offshore windmills. By 2023, Chinese producers accounted for 97 percent of domestic Chinese sales and dumped their products in foreign markets at prices 20 percent lower than those from Western competitors.

Finally, we come to electric vehicles. China produces around two-thirds of all electric vehicles and more than 80 percent of electric-battery cells, the most expensive part of the vehicles. How did they accomplish this? You guessed it, they cheated.

Perhaps you're starting to see a pattern.

The party used the familiar combination of subsidies and extortion. By handing out tens of billions of dollars in subsidies, massive tax breaks, and rebates worth more than $8,000 per car, the party turbocharged auto manufacturing and slashed the cost of its electric vehicles. China also forced global auto companies into joint ventures in return for access to the Chinese market—from Ford to Toyota to Volkswagen. Chinese companies then used these joint ventures to expand and gain access to critical technology.

After cornering the domestic Chinese market, these companies are ready to tackle the world. One company in particular is known as China's "Tesla Killer." BYD— which stands for "Build Your Dreams"—is now the world's largest electric-vehicle manufacturer thanks to billions of dollars in cheap loans, subsidies, and forced joint ventures. BYD's cheapest car costs around a third of Tesla's cheapest car given these unfair advantages. BYD is now leading China's charge into foreign markets: China exported a reported five million cars in 2023, which made it the world's largest auto exporter. With astonishing swiftness, it might be on the verge of destroying yet another American industry.

You don't need to put solar panels on your roof or drive an electric vehicle to recognize the unfairness of it all. Thousands of our fellow Americans feed their families with jobs in these industries, and they deserve a level playing field just like any other American worker. Plus, there's the danger of a green future becoming a red future. If we become too reliant on the Chinese Communist Party for our energy or other critical resources of the modern economy, we open ourselves to the whims of an imperialist Communist power. Indeed, China is already using its economic might to impose its will on other countries.

Economic Imperialism

As China has grown rich, the Chinese Communist Party has weaponized the world's second largest economy to bribe or punish other nations—sometimes both. The party controls access to its giant domestic market, leverages critical exports, sanctions its critics, and lures foreign governments into infrastructure-driven debt traps. Like everything else, the Communists see their economy as just another instrument of power for their regime.

As the second largest importer in the world, the party controls the flow of more than $3 trillion worth of foreign goods and services entering the country each year. This vast import market gives China leverage over companies and thus governments who depend on access to the Chinese market. And the party exploits this leverage ruthlessly, leaving the products of its critics to rot in the fields and rust on the docks.

No country, industry, or sector is safe from Chinese Communist pressure and retaliation. After a Chinese human-rights activist won the Nobel Peace Prize, the party banned salmon imports from Norway, which merely hosts the prize. During a dispute over the Spratly Islands, China banned bananas from the Philippines. When Canadian authorities arrested a powerful Chinese CEO, the party banned Canadian pork and canola products. After Australia opened an inquiry into the origins of the coronavirus, China stopped importing Australian cotton and beef, imposed an 80 percent tax on Australian barley, imposed taxes as high as 212 percent on Australian wine, and restricted tourism to Australia. Amid diplomatic tensions with Japan in 2023, China banned half a billion dollars in annual Japanese seafood imports.

China is especially aggressive on matters related to Taiwan. To retaliate against Taiwan for welcoming the Speaker of the House to the island, China suspended imports of certain Taiwanese fruit and fish. When a Czech official visited Taiwan, a Chinese company conspicuously canceled nearly $24 million in Czech piano purchases, nearly crippling the targeted company. After Taiwan opened a representative office—akin to an embassy for countries without formal diplomatic relations—in

Lithuania, China banned all Lithuanian imports—every single product.

The Chinese Communist Party also weaponizes foreign dependence on its huge $3.7 trillion worth of annual exports, especially its exports of critical strategic goods like rare-earth elements. During a 2010 dispute over the Senkaku Islands, China cut off Japan from its supply of rare earths, threatening to send Japanese automakers into a tailspin. In 2019, Beijing threatened to cut off America's supply, which would have wreaked havoc on everything from our oil industry to our production of military jets. (Yes, our military depends on components from China.) The Communist propaganda rag *People's Daily* warned that "the United States risks losing the supply of materials that are vital to sustaining its technological strength." In 2023, China made good on its threats and choked off the supply of germanium and gallium to undermine American and allied production of semiconductors. China also restricted exports of graphite, undercutting foreign electric-vehicle manufacturers.

On the lower end of the tech spectrum, China also controls a dangerous proportion of our medical and pharmaceutical supply chain. After China unleashed the coronavirus pandemic on the world, the Communists responded to American criticism by threatening in their state media that "the United States would sink into the hell of a novel coronavirus epidemic" without Chinese drug exports. Sadly, this threat isn't a bluff; China could cripple public health in America by withholding basic medicines from us.

The party also uses its economic power to sanction hostile foreign officials. When the European Union imposed largely symbolic sanctions in response to the Uyghur genocide, the party retaliated by sanctioning five members of the European Parliament, more than two dozen EU ambassadors, and several EU-aligned think tanks. In the summer of 2020, the party targeted eleven Americans, including me, for criticizing China's takeover of Hong Kong. I chuckled when I heard the news. Here's part of my official response: "Chinese communism is the most dangerous threat to freedom in the world, and I will never back down from fighting it. If China thinks my opposition to its Communist tyranny to date warrants these sanctions, I have two words for them: just wait."

You can count this book as a small part of my making good on that promise.

The Belt and Road Initiative

Yet nothing compares to the imperial ambitions of Xi Jinping's Belt and Road Initiative. This massive infrastructure development strategy is a modern-day version of the Silk Road trading routes of early Imperial China. Through a web of roads, railroads, pipelines, power plants, ports, and other infrastructure projects, the Chinese Communist Party wants to spread its military, economic, and political influence across Asia and Europe, gain leverage over borrowing nations, employ its workers, and enrich its companies.

The Belt and Road Initiative includes more than 150 mostly poor or middle-income nations. The initiative will likely cost at least one trillion dollars—seven times the inflation-adjusted cost of the Marshall Plan, the U.S. effort to rebuild Europe after World War II and stop the spread of communism. Unlike the Marshall Plan, though, China expects to recoup its investments and then some—all the while spreading its Communist influence.

In *The Emperor's New Road*, Jonathan Hillman explains how China has pursued a series of often fiscally unsound projects, driving host countries into crushing debt. The most infamous example occurred in Sri Lanka, a small island nation just off India's southern coast and thus key terrain for both China and its old rival India. China financed a $210 million airport and gave Sri Lanka more than $1 billion in high-interest loans to build a deep-water port. The airport ultimately averaged only seven passengers a day, and the port fared little better. When Sri Lanka predictably couldn't pay back the loans, China extorted a ninety-nine-year lease at the unprofitable but strategically located port. Unsurprisingly, a People's Liberation Army vessel was docked at the port by 2022, along with many other Chinese vessels.

Sri Lanka is far from the only example, though not all Belt and Road projects have such clear strategic value. For instance, the party also financed the poorly functioning Belgrade–Budapest rail line that will take an estimated 2,500 years to make a profit, not including maintenance fees. Montenegro's debt skyrocketed to pay for a road that will never justify its cost. China's highest-profile rail project, in eastern Africa, is often mocked as a "railway to nowhere." Beijing doesn't plan to militarize that railroad; nor does it plan to build a military base in the Balkans—not yet, at least.

One might ask why China pursues such ill-advised projects lacking in strategic value. One obvious answer is simple influence, leverage, and stockpiling of favors. Like Vito Corleone in *The Godfather*, the party essentially says to the leaders of these countries, "Someday, and that day may never come, I will call upon you to do a service for me." Whether it is, say, a vote at the World Health Organization or a refusal to cooperate with the United States at a critical moment, the Belt and Road Initiative buys future service to the party.

Another, often overlooked, reason is that China directs much of the economic benefits back to itself. Chinese contractors build the projects, manufacturers supply the materials, and workers get many of the jobs. For example, China sent tens of thousands of its own workers to build a railroad in Laos, hiring barely seven thousand Laotians. In projects across Africa, its workers take the best jobs and then leave locals with the low-paying, menial, and often dangerous tasks. In many places, Chinese workers live and eat in closed compounds, even denying local restaurants and shops the benefit of their presence. Governments around the world use infrastructure projects to stimulate their economies; China uses Belt and Road projects in other countries to stimulate its own economy.

China's economic imperialism has harmed countries the world over, from saddling them with Belt and Road debt or hollowing out their industries with its cheating and gangster tactics. But no nation has suffered more harm than ours.

Though it might seem odd at first that the world's wealthiest and most powerful nation has suffered the most from China's economic aggression, it makes sense when you think about it. First, the United States has had the most to lose from China's depredations, not some small and poor country. Second, the Chinese Communist Party knew it had to knock the United States off its pedestal to achieve its goal of global dominance. And that's what it aimed to do—sadly abetted by foolish decisions to grant China permanent most-favored-nation status and welcome it into the World Trade Organization.

Since then, China has inflicted a severe and enduring depression on U.S. manufacturing. We've lost tens of thousands of factories and more than four million manufacturing jobs—nearly a quarter of all manufacturing jobs. Those losses then rippled through communities, shuttering restaurants, shops, and other small businesses. Too often, drug and alcohol abuse soared and suicide rates spiked; tragically, the communities most devastated by China's economic world war soon became ground zero for China's reverse opioid war (more on that in chapter 6). Boarded-up neighborhoods, empty main streets, and rusting factories stand as stark reminders of this economic disaster.

The worst geopolitical mistake in American history may have been granting China permanent most-favored-nation status and allowing it to enter the World Trade Organization. We built up our most formidable enemy and empowered it to devastate our economy and threaten our national security. What's more, America's economic opening to China didn't increase our influence over them; it increased China's influence over us. The Chinese Communist Party has infiltrated America and now has an army of puppets, allies, and useful idiots in our midst.

China Has Infiltrated Our Society

Just as Chinese Communists have extorted and shaken down foreign governments, so, too, have they compromised American businessmen, academics, and celebrities. China uses greed and fear to influence our elite, harnessing its economic power to send a simple message: Stay quiet about our crimes and we'll make you rich. Speak out and we'll destroy you.

China has given our elites far more than thirty pieces of silver, but everything comes at a price. In return for vast wealth, these elites bend the knee to Communist China and often act as de facto accomplices in Beijing's crimes. And it cuts across all segments of American society.

Hollywood

Let's start with Hollywood's notorious kowtowing to China, which has muzzled America's most popular art form and brought actors, directors, and studio executives to heel. As a result, Hollywood hasn't released a movie featuring China as the villain in more than a generation.

The Chinese Communist Party effectively conquered Hollywood in 1997. Sony Pictures released *Seven Years in Tibet*, starring Brad Pitt, and Disney released the Martin Scorsese–directed *Kundun*. Both films criticized China's genocide in Tibet and favorably portrayed the Dalai Lama. China retaliated furiously, banning Disney- and Sony-affiliated Columbia Tristar from China, barring Scorsese and Pitt from traveling to China, and threatening to expel all Sony employees from the country. Instead of standing by their films and their supposed principles, both companies buckled. Disney suppressed the release of *Kundun*, opening the film in just two theaters on Christmas Day. Disney's CEO, Michael Eisner, traveled to Beijing for a groveling apology, calling the film a "stupid mistake." Sony tried to buy absolution by lobbying for China's entry into the World Trade Organization and plying Chinese officials with gifts.

This self-abasement ultimately earned Disney and Sony a reprieve from China, and earned China billions of dollars in investment from both companies, but the precedent was set. The party proved that it could and would throttle major Hollywood studios that crossed it. And the party has maintained a boot on Hollywood's neck ever since, strictly controlling what films are released in China's massive and lucrative movie market. China can also imperil other studio assets inside its borders, like Disney's theme parks in Shanghai and Hong Kong.

This story and its lasting consequences of "preemptive obedience" are told in Erich Schwartzel's *Red Carpet: Hollywood, China, and the Global Battle for Cultural Supremacy.* These days, Chinese censors rarely need to suppress movies because American filmmakers do it themselves. Movie projects casting even the slightest aspersions on China rarely escape the planning stages.

But such movies still occasionally bubble to the surface, with results both telling and comedic. Consider, for instance, MGM's 2012 remake of the 1984 Cold War classic *Red Dawn.* In the original film, heroic American teenagers fight to protect their community and country after a Russian invasion. In the remake, the young Americans battle a Chinese invasion—that is, until MGM's executives intervened. Fearing Chinese retaliation, they digitally altered Chinese flags and insignia and made North Korea the invading bad guys instead of China. Who would've imagined that an impoverished, starving nation of just twenty-five million people could conquer vast portions of America with its fleet of fishing dinghies? Hollywood execs, that's who, if that's what it takes to do business with Communist China.

Other examples abound. The makers of the 2013 movie *World War Z* changed the origin of a zombie outbreak from China (as it was in the book of the same name) to

North Korea. After all, who could believe that a global viral pandemic could start in China?

In the Marvel blockbuster *Doctor Strange*, the British actress Tilda Swinton plays the role of "the Ancient One," who in the Marvel comic books has Tibetan origins, but in the movie does not. One of the film's screenwriters explained the decision to sanitize the character: "If you acknowledge that Tibet is a place and that he's Tibetan, you risk alienating one billion people . . . and risk the Chinese government going, 'Hey, you know one of the biggest film-watching countries in the world? We're not going to show your movie because you decided to get political.'" As if self-censorship weren't the actual "political" decision. And Marvel, of course, is owned by Disney.

Hollywood even lends subtle support for Communist China's controversial policies. For instance, Disney infamously filmed the 2020 movie *Mulan* in Xinjiang and during the end credits thanked eight Chinese government entities, including the public-security bureau of a city operating more than a dozen concentration camps. Another common practice is needlessly displaying the "nine-dash line," a preposterous map outlining China's spurious claims to the entirety of the South China Sea, including the territorial waters of every other nation bordering the sea. The 2019 animated children's movie *Abominable* and the 2022 movie *Uncharted* featured a version of the nine-dash line, and the 2023 blockbuster *Barbie* appeared to as well. In response, various combinations of the Philippines, Malaysia, and Vietnam banned the movies from their countries.

With "preemptive obedience" the order of the day, China expects abject apologies from any Hollywood figure who missteps. In 2021, for example, the actor John Cena inadvertently referred to Taiwan as a "country" while promoting the release of *Fast & Furious 9*. Fearing that China might ban the film, he released a video begging forgiveness in Mandarin, "I made a mistake, I must say right now. It's so so so so so so important, I love and respect Chinese people. I'm very sorry for my mistakes. Sorry. Sorry. I'm really sorry. You have to understand that I love and respect China and Chinese people."

Mao described the Communist perspective on art succinctly when he said that there is "no such thing as art for art's sake." Xi Jinping has added that "the literary and art front is a vital front of the Party and the people." Like everything else, art is simply another tool to strengthen the party's rule. What's remarkable is that the Communists have warped not only Chinese art to this purpose, but American art as well. Unfortunately, the same is increasingly the case with American sports.

Professional Sports

Like Hollywood stars, American sports stars enjoy outsize cultural status, and many don't hesitate to express social, moral, and political opinions. Communist China thus not only threatens them if they criticize China, but also enlists them as Chinese mouthpieces.

As with Hollywood, the sports world had its own singular moment when China's influence broke into the open. During China's crackdown in Hong Kong in 2019, Houston Rockets general manager Daryl Morey tweeted "Fight for Freedom. Stand with Hong Kong." China, where the NBA is very popular, struck back harshly. The party pulled all NBA games from state television. Tencent, a massive state-influenced company, suspended its news and streaming services about the Rockets. Chinese retailers stopped selling Rockets sneakers and jerseys. The Chinese Basketball Association suspended all cooperation with the Rockets. All told, the party inflicted an estimated $400 million in damages on American basketball.

The NBA didn't fight back, but rather rolled over to appease the Chinese Communist Party. Morey felt compelled to delete his tweet and issued an apologetic statement. Rockets owner Tilman Fertitta tweeted that Morey "does NOT speak for" the Houston Rockets. And the NBA lamented that "the views expressed by Houston Rockets General Manager Daryl Morey have deeply offended many of our friends and fans in China."

Communist apologists in the league piled on. Most notably, Lebron James condemned Morey and excused China, saying that Morey was "either misinformed or not really educated on the situation" and adding that "yes, we do have freedom of speech, but there can be a lot of negative that comes with that, too." No word from James about the "negative" for Hong Kongers trying to exercise their freedom of speech. Golden State Warriors coach Steve Kerr also defended the Chinese Communists, given that "none of us are perfect, and we all have different issues." He then compared Americans "owning AR-15s and mowing each other down in a mall" to China's crackdown in Hong Kong, an insult both to law-abiding American gun owners and to the brave Hong Kongers fighting for their freedom. All too typical, American celebrities will speak out for liberal, woke causes but will remain silent—and demand silence from others—on Chinese Communist atrocities.

Meanwhile, the NBA's broadcast partner ESPN—which is owned by Disney, by the way—refused to defend Morey. ESPN reportedly issued a gag order, "mandating that any discussion of the Daryl Morey story avoid any political discussions about China and Hong Kong." But that directive didn't stop one of ESPN's star commentators, Stephen A. Smith, from publicly lecturing Morey, "You have an obligation to adopt and embrace the interest of those you collect a paycheck from." This nicely sums up China's influence strategy: Don't bite the hand that feeds you.

But the Chinese Communists weren't satisfied; they demanded that the NBA fire Morey. While the NBA commissioner claims that he refused the ultimatum, con-

veniently enough, Morey was out of his job within barely
a year. Two months later, the Rockets were back on the
air in China. Nor was Morey the only one to lose his job.
The Brooklyn Nets CEO, David Levy, had the audacity
to defend Morey and say, "Whatever corporation you're
in or country you live in, you should remain loyal to the
values you have. Period." And then he "resigned" after
fewer than two months on the job—which isn't surprising:
the Nets' owner is Joe Tsai, a founder of the Chinese retail
giant Alibaba and a frequent apologist for the Chinese
Communist Party.

Two years later, the party again flexed its economic
muscle, this time against the Turkish American Boston
Celtics player Enes Kanter Freedom. Enes, who changed
his last name to Freedom when he became a natural-
ized citizen in 2021, is a champion of human rights, not
only in Turkey, but also in China. And Enes didn't keep
his advocacy secret: he called Xi Jinping a "dictator" and
wore shoes emblazoned with the words "Free Tibet."
As with the Rockets, Tencent stopped streaming Celtics
games and deleted Celtics games in its archive. I've gotten
to know Enes on his regular trips to Washington, and he
later shared with me that team officials and even his own
players union pressured him not to wear the shoes and to
stop criticizing China. Not only did he bravely refuse,
but he proceeded to wear other shoes highlighting the
Uyghur genocide, China's use of slave labor, and Taiwan's
freedom. A few months later, the Celtics traded him to

the Houston Rockets. Perhaps unsurprisingly, given the Rockets' experience with Morey, they immediately released him, and he hasn't played since. Freedom believes, as do I, that he was blacklisted from the NBA because of his criticism of China.

Even before these twin controversies, the NBA had curried favor with China in other ways, for instance, by opening a youth training facility in Xinjiang. The NBA kept the facility open long after the Uyghur genocide was common knowledge; indeed, the league closed the facility only following credible reports of abuse there. The NBA didn't even mention the genocide occurring within driving distance of its facility.

China is also extending its reach to other sports leagues. The party-controlled Tencent signed streaming deals with ESPN in 2016, the NFL in 2017, and MLB in 2018. Even if they avoid the NBA's public controversies, each of them knows that China can and likely will inflict massive financial damages if their employees or players step out of line.

The party has also laid down the law with foreign soccer teams popular in America. After Arsenal player Mesut Özil criticized the party's genocide in Xinjiang, Beijing temporarily pulled Arsenal matches from the air, removed Özil's avatar from video games, and made it impossible to search for his name on the internet. Predictably, Arsenal took China's side, and within ten months, Özil was no longer playing. While Arsenal denies that it effectively benched him for his anti-China comments, Özil insists that moment was when his professional descent began. It certainly fits a pattern—few critics of China seem to keep their jobs.

But the Chinese Communist Party isn't satisfied with simply silencing and manipulating America's cultural figures; it wants to tame all of American media.

News Media

China cultivates and extorts American celebrities and athletes, enlisting them to minimize China's crimes and rally support for the Chinese Communists. By the same token, China fears the potential of American media even more and thus strives to intimidate it and control the flow of information about China. Sadly, the party too often succeeds.

Though China can't extort American media as it does the NBA or Hollywood studios—it already bans American news—the owners of media companies aren't immune from pressure. Consider that Disney, Comcast, Warner Bros. Discovery, and Paramount Global own ABC, NBC, CNN, and CBS, respectively. As we've seen, these companies have billions of dollars to lose if their media subsidiaries step out of line. Do you trust them not to pull punches for China? I sure don't. By contrast, Fox News is the only major news network not owned by a parent company susceptible to Chinese pressure, and its coverage is by far the most critical of China. Compare that with CNN's owner, Warner Bros. Discovery, which partnered in 2021 with a Communist propaganda outlet to produce a documentary on Xinjiang that omitted any mention of the Uyghur genocide.

And major news networks aren't the only media companies vulnerable to extortion through their corporate parents. After Bloomberg News ran an exposé revealing Communist Party corruption in 2012, the party blocked its website and retaliated by restricting sales of Bloomberg's highly profitable software systems in the country. Lesson learned. The next year, Bloomberg News refused to run another corruption story and fired the author of the piece. Bloomberg lawyers even tried to threaten the reporter's wife into signing a nondisclosure agreement. Michael Bloomberg himself led by example, declaring in 2019 that "Xi Jinping is not a dictator" and that the Chinese Communists "listen to the public." When he ran for president in 2020, the billionaire promised to deescalate trade tensions with Beijing and attacked "Trump's trade war" against China.

Similarly, *Forbes* began censoring anti-Communist content shortly after a Hong Kong company purchased the magazine in 2014. One *Forbes* editor declared that it's "not accurate to say that China impoverishes its people or to label Xi Jinping a dictator." The magazine also stopped publishing editorials by prominent China critic Gordon Chang and removed his previous articles from the website. In both 2021 and 2023, Communist-linked firms tried to buy *Forbes* outright. I fought those purchases in the Senate, but it seems they don't need to own *Forbes* to control it.

And in 2023, Apple TV canceled the Emmy-nominated show *The Problem with Jon Stewart* over editorial disputes with Stewart, most notably about China. Not coincidently, Apple has extensive business ties with China both as a manufacturing site and a market for its products. Apple CEO Tim Cook has acknowledged, "There's no supply chain in the world more critical to Apple than that of China."

The party also literally buys influence in American media, spending millions of dollars to insert propaganda articles from *China Daily* in newspapers such as the *Washington Post*, the *New York Times*, and the *Financial Times*. From 2011 through 2019, *China Daily* purchased at least five hundred pages of ads designed to look like news articles in six of America's most influential papers. If you've ever seen an article under the banner "China Watch," just know that it's Communist propaganda.

Chinese propaganda may be seeping into American news in subtler ways as well. In 2018, China's government-run news agency Xinhua signed a cooperation agreement with the Associated Press, a commonly trusted news source, especially for state and local newspapers. Though the AP minimizes the agreement, Xinhua tells a much rosier tale, claiming that "cooperation between the two news agencies has kept expanding and deepening since 1972" and that "the two news agencies have broad co-operation." Neither Xinhua nor the AP has released the agreement, leaving Americans unsure if the AP's coverage favors the Chinese Communist Party.

Another tool the party uses to shape American media coverage is its stranglehold on information coming out of China. With its conquest of Hong Kong in 2020, the party crushed the final refuge of free press on the mainland. It fired, imprisoned, and intimidated the journalists and bookstore owners who had once provided insights and original reporting on the party to the outside world. And the Western journalists now allowed in China face its usual tools of influence and intimidation. In 2019, for example, Chinese authorities refused to renew the visa of a *Wall Street Journal* reporter in retaliation for his co-authoring an article about the criminal activities of Xi Jinping's cousin. In 2020, the party expelled three more *Journal* reporters after the paper published an article titled "China Is the Real Sick Man of Asia."

Nor does the party rest with the news out of China; it's also buying up Chinese-language news outlets around the world. In *Hidden Hand*, Clive Hamilton and Mareike Ohlberg write, "As a result of concerted efforts by Beijing, nearly all Chinese-language media in Western countries are now directly or effectively under CCP control." The most prized acquisition occurred when the Communist billionaire Jack Ma purchased the prominent Hong Kong–based *South China Morning Post*, which was once a trusted source of news out of China.

China's creeping influence over our media comes from a combination of intimidation, cooperation, and censorship. But with our universities and colleges, which so heavily influence the trends and tastes in our media and thus our broader society, China has also found willing partners.

Higher Education

One might think that with mottoes like "Truth" (Harvard), "Light and Truth" (Yale), and "Let There Be Light" (University of California), our universities might be natural and potent enemies of the Chinese Communist Party, but far from it. The ideological rot that besets their campuses, along with cold hard Chinese cash, has turned many in the academy into accomplices and apologists for the worst human-rights abuser in the world.

In the 2022–2023 school year, 290,000 Chinese students studied in the United States, the largest foreign student population on American campuses. Over the years, these students have ranged from normal middle-income Chinese to Xi Jinping's daughter to more than 2,500 scientists and engineers sponsored by the Chinese military. Nearly half of China's students in the United States are studying science, technology, engineering, and mathematics. It's no exaggeration to say that we're teaching China's youth how to build the technologies of tomorrow, enabling China to threaten our security and prosperity. If you ask me, China needs to learn the *Federalist Papers* from us, not artificial intelligence and quantum computing.

But most universities don't mind, because these students typically pay full freight, with annual tuition revenue reaching nearly $15 billion in 2018. As we've seen, though, everything from China comes at a price. The University of California, San Diego, learned this lesson in 2017, when China froze scholarships for Chinese students at the school after it invited the Dalai Lama to speak. No small blow to UC San Diego, where one in seven students was Chinese.

Though tuition revenue is the largest, it's far from the only source of Chinese cash for America's campuses. China has donated at least $1 billion to our universities since 2013, but the true amount is probably much higher. Despite a federal law requiring disclosure of foreign gifts, the Department of Education has found that universities systematically underreported more than $6.5 billion in foreign donations. And these donations usually come with strings attached. For example, Joe Tsai—the China apologist and Brooklyn Nets owner whose team CEO lost his job after defending Daryl Morey—donated $30 million to Yale for the Paul Tsai China Center. Not surprisingly, as Peter Schweizer details in *Red-Handed*, the Tsai Center frequently hosts Chinese officials, defends the party's policies, and whitewashes its crimes.

China also plies American academics with lucrative contracts. In 2021, American universities signed $120 million worth of deals with Chinese entities, including the Chinese government itself. A *Wall Street Journal* analysis of publicly disclosed contracts estimated the total value at more than $2.3 billion between 2012 and 2024. For example, Stanford, MIT, and the University of California, Berkeley, had contracts with the Chinese telecom giant Huawei, which our government has blacklisted for its close ties to Chinese intelligence. And again, the true amount is probably higher given the lax disclosure by many universities.

Another avenue of influence was so-called Confucius Institutes on American campuses. China spent more than $158 million between 2006 and 2019 to create these supposed Chinese-language and cultural-exchange centers. In reality, the institutes were little more than beachheads of Communist influence. A Senate committee found that "the Chinese government approves all teachers, events, and speakers" at Confucius Institutes and that "some U.S. schools contractually agree that both Chinese and U.S. laws will apply." Institute employees silenced anti-Communist speakers, tore down posters critical of China, and spread party propaganda to America's youth. In 2009, North Carolina State University even canceled a visit by the Dalai Lama after its Confucius Institute director said the visit might harm the "strong relationships we were developing with China."

Fortunately, these Communist outposts have now largely been shut down. In 2020, the Trump administration designated Confucius Institutes as "foreign missions," and Congress later prohibited Department of Defense funding to any university hosting a Confucius Institute. As a result, only ten institutes remained by 2023. On one hand, the presence of nearly 120 Confucius Institutes across America demonstrated China's influence and our universities' complicity. On the other, the shuttering of most of them proves that we're capable of combating this influence.

Sometimes the party's campus tactics cross into the outright criminal. In particular, China's Thousand Talents Plan recruits and pays scholars to steal technology from their universities. In 2020, for example, the Department of Justice arrested the chair of Harvard's chemistry and chemical biology department for taking $50,000 a month from China while also working on projects for the Department of Defense and the National Institutes of Health. The Department of Justice has also prosecuted professors from, among others, Emory University, Texas A&M, West Virginia University, and Ohio State University. The University of Arkansas professor whose arrest I mentioned in the previous chapter also participated in China's talent programs.

Through its embassy and consulates, China also bankrolls and controls Chinese student groups on campuses—most notably, the Chinese Students and Scholars Association. In both 2012 and 2015, Chinese diplomats and the association organized adoring crowds to welcome Xi Jinping when he visited Washington—a worrisome ability to organize large, pro-Communist crowds in our nation's capital. On campus, the approximately 150 association chapters are even more aggressive; they harass China's critics, spy on classmates, and promote Chinese-funded projects near campus. In 2022, the association even convinced George Washington University to rip down posters critical of that year's Beijing Olympics by claiming the posters were "racist." I suppose even Chinese Communists know that campus liberals are easy marks for such bogus accusations.

The Chinese Communist Party has corrupted many of our institutions of higher education. But its influence on campuses pales in comparison to its influence in America's boardrooms.

Corporate America

The Chinese Communist Party has used its familiar combination of greed and fear to enlist corporate America under its banner. To be frank, though, it didn't take much. Too many American corporations happily jumped at the chance to make a killing in China. They've done everything from helping to build China's Orwellian police state to employing its slaves to legitimizing its ominous territorial claims.

Before Chinese companies mastered the cutting edge of surveillance technology, the party turned to Americans for help to control its subjects. Seeing a massive market, American technology companies jumped at the chance. Cisco provided routers that enabled the party to restrict key words and block web pages. Microsoft developed a blogging software that censored forbidden political terms. IBM helped to design "smart cities" technologies to monitor and centrally control every detail of city life. American semiconductor makers Intel and Nvidia provided advanced microchips to the Xinjiang Supercomputing Center, which can reportedly search one hundred million photos a second. As late as 2019, Google was working on Project Dragonfly—aptly named after the insect with thousands of eyes—to design a censored search engine for China's government. Just last year, the party ordered Apple to remove the encrypted messaging apps Signal, Telegram, and WhatsApp from its App Store in China. With its bottom line so dependent on China, Apple meekly complied.

Now Beijing has even used American technology companies to extend its censorship into the United States. In *Beijing Rules*, Bethany Allen details how LinkedIn and Zoom help the party silence and monitor its political enemies abroad. Zoom employees disrupted the accounts of Chinese dissidents, provided the personal information of users participating in online Tiananmen Square memorial services, and handed over the account names and user IDs for 23,000 Zoom accounts connected to people from Xinjiang. At LinkedIn—where a senior official described the Chinese government as "a key stakeholder"— the company censored academics and journalists who discussed hot-button issues like the Tiananmen Square Massacre. LinkedIn repeatedly recommended that wayward foreigners "update" their opinions so as not to offend the Communists.

Chasing Chinese dollars, America's tech titans have also shamefully supplicated China's Communist rulers. Microsoft founder Bill Gates praised China's dictator, saying that "I am impressed [with] how hard President Xi works . . . he's quite amazing." Facebook CEO Mark Zuckerberg bought copies of Xi's book *The Governance of China* and gave them to his employees because "I want them to understand socialism with Chinese characteristics." At a White House State Dinner honoring Xi the next year, Zuckerberg bizarrely asked the Communist dictator to name his unborn daughter. Elon Musk told China's state television, "I'm very confident that the future of China is going to be great and that China is headed towards being the biggest economy in the world and a lot of prosperity in the future."

But Silicon Valley isn't the only accomplice in China's

crimes: a shocking number of American companies are complicit in the party's use of Uyghur slave labor. According to a 2020 congressional investigation, Nike, Coca-Cola, Adidas, Calvin Klein, Campbell Soup Company, Costco, Patagonia, and Tommy Hilfiger all likely employed forced labor in their supply chains. The companies claimed ignorance of the use of this slave labor, but that ignorance was likely deliberate. After all, Coca-Cola, Nike, and Apple lobbied later that year against a law blocking imports made with Chinese slave labor.

Which shouldn't be surprising: During that investigation, I grilled a Coca-Cola executive—who was in charge of human rights, no less—about the Uyghur genocide. He dodged and dissembled so embarrassingly that he clearly had orders not to say anything that would offend the Chinese Communists. Likewise, Nike's lobbying should come as no surprise, given that its then CEO, John Donahoe, said in 2021 that "Nike is a brand that is of China and for China." When it comes to Chinese genocide, maybe Nike's slogan is "Just Do It."

The party also bullies American companies into legitimizing its bogus territorial claims. In 2018, for example, it blocked Marriott's website and app in China after learning the company listed Tibet, Hong Kong, and Taiwan on a drop-down menu of countries. Marriott abjectly issued a groveling apology: "We absolutely will not support any separatist organization that will undermine China's sovereignty and territorial integrity." That same year, it fired a Nebraska employee for accidentally liking a tweet about Tibet. The forty-nine-year-old told reporters that "this job was all I had." In 2021, the hotel remained so afraid of Chinese retaliation that it also refused to host a convention of Uyghur activists. Chinese authorities similarly pressured forty-four international airlines—including United, American, and Delta—to remove Taiwan from destination menus. America's leading airlines now list only the island's capital city of Taipei to avoid offending the Communists. And in 2018, Gap had to "sincerely apologize" for a shirt featuring a map of China that didn't include Taiwan, the nine-dash line, or disputed territory with India. Gap regretted that its shirt "failed to reflect the correct map of China," even though it was perfectly accurate.

The sad truth is that too many of our largest companies have too often aided and abetted our deadliest enemy. And too many on Wall Street have worked hand in glove with corporate America and the Chinese Communist Party to bankroll them both.

Wall Street

Our nation's financial and professional elites have either hatched or supported nearly every one of Washington's bad decisions, rosy projections, and long-winded excuses for our flawed China policy. When they look at China's

massive economy, 1.4 billion subjects, and growing industrial might, they see only opportunities, never threats. These
days, after all, even Communists need bankers, investors,
and consultants.

In 2020, U.S. investors held an estimated $1.2 trillion
in Chinese stocks and bonds, and Wall Street's biggest
banks held the biggest positions. In recent years, Bank of
America, Citigroup, JPMorganChase, and Morgan Stanley alone have invested between $45 and $65 billion in
China. Goldman Sachs doubled its annual financing for
Chinese companies and government agencies between
2018 and 2020 to $17.5 billion. Of course, this direct in-
vestment only scratches the surface of these banks' exposure to China, because they also finance the multinational
corporations operating there.

Moreover, American banks, private-equity firms, and
hedge funds aren't just investing in blue jeans, toys, and
fake Christmas trees; they've also underwritten the Chinese Communist Party's key strategic priorities. American hedge funds bankrolled the construction of China's
surveillance state. American venture capitalists invested
tens of billions of dollars into cutting-edge Chinese artificial intelligence. Warren Buffett's famed Berkshire
Capital invested heavily and early in electric vehicle giant
BYD. In 2023, BlackRock had nearly $430 million in-
vested in blacklisted Chinese companies, while Morgan
Stanley was invested in more than forty companies tied
to human rights abuses or the People's Liberation Army.

To win even more business in China, many Wall Street banks hired the friends and families of senior Communist officials. JPMorganChase even had a "Sons and Daughters" program for the Communist elite, hiring around one hundred princelings. This program flagrantly violated American anti-corruption laws, for which JPMorganChase paid a $264 million fine. Goldman Sachs put Jiang Zemin's grandson on its payroll. Merrill Lynch made the son-in-law of the former chairman of the National People's Congress its vice chairman of China investment banking. While Wall Street hired these unqualified princelings to influence the party, the influence game runs in both directions.

The Chinese Communist Party knows that it can reliably call on America's financial elites to advance its interests. I saw these efforts in action during the Trump administration. As trade tensions intensified in 2018, the party's top trade negotiator summoned top Wall Street executives to a luxury hotel across the street from the White House to deliver a simple message: "We need your help." The executives answered the call: in return for promises of greater access to the Chinese market, they furiously lobbied the White House and Congress on China's behalf. I heard from several Trump administration officials frustrated by the intensity of the campaign. Peter Navarro, a White House trade advisor, fumed publicly that "globalist billionaires" were acting as China's "unpaid foreign agents." And the efforts didn't stop when Joe

Biden took office, with the president's exasperated national security advisor sniping that "our priority is not to get access for Goldman Sachs in China."

Most Wall Street heavyweights don't hide their sympathy for the Chinese regime. BlackRock's Larry Fink is Wall Street's high priest of political correctness, extolling diversity and trying to cut off investment funds from gun manufacturers and fossil-fuel companies. But his moral conscience doesn't extend to China. He has showered Xi Jinping with praise: "I would qualify the Chinese leadership as one of the best leadership teams in the world." Fink has also observed, "In theory, some elements of the society may have less rights, but on the other hand, I would say the majority of society in China have done very well." In other words, toe the line and you'll do fine. But if you're Tibetan, Uyghur, Christian, Muslim, Falun Gong, or anti-Communist, well, you'll just have to make do with fewer rights, according to Larry Fink.

But Fink is far from the only Chinese apologist on Wall Street. As late as 2023, Citigroup CEO Jane Fraser declared that China was still safe for investment and would produce strong returns: "The next China," she said, "is China." Warren Buffett's longtime business partner, billionaire Charlie Munger, opined, "I would argue their system has worked better for them than ours has for us." Munger praised Xi Jinping when he disappeared billionaire Jack Ma for criticizing the government, chuckling that the "Communists did the right thing" and lamenting that American regulators didn't behave more like China's Communist regime.

Charlie Munger was among America's most respected investors, yet he displayed a revolting moral equivalence about China—in fact, he seemed to favor many features of the Communist system. Sadly, given how Wall Street financed China's rise, it seems that Munger was respected not in spite of his views on China, but in part *because* of them.

∗ ∗ ∗

The Chinese Communist Party has insinuated itself into almost every corner of American society. Chinese Communist influence has warped, censored, or defiled something important in your life—whether it's your entertainment, news sources, alma mater, employer, bank, or retirement fund. Contrary to the promises of so many that China would democratize if we helped it grow rich, the Chinese Communist Party has become more aggressive and has used its riches to influence and subvert our country.

And perhaps worst of all, they've also infiltrated our government.

||||||||||||||||||||||||||||||||

China Has Infiltrated
Our Government

The Chinese Communist Party doesn't merely corrupt our cultural, economic, and academic institutions, but also targets our government at every level. You might suspect a Communist rival, naturally, to spy on the military or the CIA, but that your small state or hometown is of no concern to China. Unfortunately, you would be wrong.

Through a mix of traditional espionage, influence peddling, and other underhanded means, the Chinese Communists strive to defeat the United States from within every day. They have spied on our military, stolen our weapons technology, courted state and local politicians, and cultivated a powerful New China Lobby in Washington to pressure your elected representatives. China wants to turn the servants of the American people into yet more servants of the Chinese Communist Party.

Targeting Our Military

The U.S. military is the single biggest obstacle to Communist China's global ambitions, hence also a top target of Chinese espionage. From old-fashioned spy work and bribes to computer hacks to physical intrusions, China uses every tool in the box against our military.

Though our troops are almost invariably patriotic, honorable, and incorruptible, it's a sad truth that any organization as large as our military will have a few bad apples—and China ruthlessly seeks them out to subvert the military. In 2024, for example, an Army intelligence analyst was charged with transferring vast amounts of classified information to a Chinese agent, including information related to our plans to defend Taiwan from a Chinese attack. In exchange, he pocketed $42,000. The year before, two sailors were arrested for turning over sensitive information about U.S. naval vessels, radar systems in Japan, and military exercises in the Pacific for less than $20,000.

China also tries to enlist our veterans to its cause once they leave our military. In 2017, the Department of Justice indicted a former Marine Corps weapons-and-tactics flight instructor who had renounced his citizenship, moved his family to China, and trained Chinese military pilots for more than $100,000. By 2024, our government was still seeking his extradition. Also in

2017, a logistics-and-security company led by American veterans started security training programs for thousands of Chinese military personnel and police officers, while also providing security for Belt and Road Initiative projects around the world. The U.S. Department of Commerce subsequently blacklisted the company because of the training it provided to the Chinese military.

The party also steals critical military secrets from America's defense companies, using a combination of economic leverage, bribes, cyber hacks, and other traditional spycraft. In return for promises of greater market access in the 1990s, Hughes Electronics transferred to China space technology, which could also be used to develop intercontinental ballistic missiles. In the early 2000s, Chinese operatives bribed a former Northrop Grumman engineer to provide information about our B-2 stealth bomber and to help design a Chinese stealth cruise missile. From 2008 to 2014, Chinese hackers pilfered Boeing's design secrets for the F-22 and F-35 stealth fighters, along with our C-17 cargo aircraft; China likely used these secrets to design its own Xi'an Y-20 cargo ship and J-20 stealth fighter. In 2018, Chinese hackers stole highly sensitive information from another military contractor, including a secret plan to develop a submarine-launched supersonic anti-ship missile. In 2024, Boeing was fined $51 million after its China-based employees downloaded data about its fighter jets, helicopters, and missile systems at least twenty-five times.

China also supplements these traditional tactics with LinkedIn, a novel way to identify and recruit thousands of potential targets. Through the platform, its agents recruited a General Electric Aviation engineer to steal jet-engine technology and a former Central Intelligence Agency employee to turn over the identities of U.S. sources. LinkedIn is particularly useful to Chinese intelligence because the app indicates when targets are out of work and, hence, most vulnerable to recruitment.

Chinese spies trolling social media for down-on-their-luck tech workers is a good example of the party's so-called "thousand grains of sand" approach to intelligence gathering. In his book *Spies and Lies*, Alex Joske offers a vivid analogy:

> the "grains of sand" analogy explains that if Russia needed to gather a thousand grains of sand from a beach (that is, a thousand grains of intelligence), it would send a submarine to deploy a highly trained team of clandestine agents to shovel up sand in the dead of night. In contrast, China would send a stream of tourists to the beach in broad daylight, each picking up a single grain. Back in Beijing, each grain of sand is then analysed and aggregated to form a brilliant picture.

In addition to its sophisticated, high-tech methods, the party still deploys plenty of low-tech methods of spying as well. One prime example is so-called gate-crashing, the increasingly common occurrence of Chinese nationals (while often pretending to be confused tourists) attempting to drive onto our military bases. On one occasion, Chinese nationals tried to push past military guards at Fort Wainwright, in Alaska, insisting they had a nonexistent reservation at a nonexistent hotel on base. Military guards have also caught Chinese nationals scuba diving off Cape Canaveral, near the Kennedy Space Center, swimming near and taking pictures of an intelligence center in Key West, and crossing into a missile range in New Mexico. Two Chinese diplomats and their wives even drove onto a base in Virginia where Navy SEALs train, resulting in the Trump administration expelling them from the country.

Chinese proxies are also buying up American farmland, often near our military bases. In North Dakota, for instance, a Chinese company purchased three hundred acres of farmland a few miles from the Grand Forks Air Force Base. The local government at first welcomed the project and the jobs it would bring, partly because Air Force officials hesitated to state their concerns publicly. But I understood the threat, as did the state's congressional delegation, especially given that the company planned a curiously tall corn mill that would've extended its line of sight far into the base. We pressed Air Force officials to speak out. Once they did, the city council voted to cancel the project, to chants of "U.S.A.!" from local citizens in the audience.

Nor was Grand Forks an isolated instance. In Texas, a former Chinese military official purchased more than 130,000 acres near the Air Force's largest pilot training base. There, too, the Chinese owners planned unusually tall structures—a field of windmills—that would have conveniently enhanced potential surveillance opportunities. In my opinion, foreign nationals of hostile countries shouldn't own a single square inch of American farmland, but they especially shouldn't own anything near our sensitive military bases.

Perhaps most infamously, Chinese intelligence is also targeting our military from above. In 2023, China floated a two-hundred-foot-tall and two-thousand-pound spy balloon over nearly the entire length of the continental United States. The balloon hovered particularly over Malmstrom Air Force Base in Montana, where our military controls more than one hundred intercontinental ballistic missiles and other nuclear assets. Notably, this same military base is surrounded by cell-phone towers equipped with Chinese technology, which could also serve intelligence-gathering purposes.

China has targeted our military and is watching it from within, around, and above. But in most cases, at least, the Americans involved were unwitting innocents. The same cannot be said, alas, for China's infiltration of the Washington swamp.

The Washington Swamp

In Washington, the Chinese Communist Party doesn't have to hack or trick Americans—it usually just buys them off. Too many politicians, bureaucrats, and their ilk suffer from willful blindness at best or naked greed more commonly. The result is a New China Lobby paralyzing Washington, as Chinese Communists wage economic war and prepare for actual war.

China does, of course, have actual spies in Washington. After the 1996 election, for example, the Democratic National Committee had to return more than $2.8 million from Chinese agents and military intelligence. The scandal resulted in nearly two dozen criminal convictions. In another case, Chinese double agent Katrina Leung, over more than a decade, received $1.7 million from the FBI, slept with at least two FBI agents, and stole classified material, including information about a highly classified counterintelligence program.

Chinese agents have also insinuated themselves into key political circles. Senator Dianne Feinstein employed a Chinese spy for around two decades—even as Feinstein served on and chaired the Senate Intelligence Committee.

The spy worked as her driver, her liaison with San Francisco's Chinese community, and her representative at the Chinese consulate. Eric Swalwell, a California congressman and a former member of the House Intelligence Committee, also had a close relationship with a Chinese spy, Christine Fang. She befriended Swalwell, raised money for his campaign, and apparently had a romantic relationship with him. In 2022, Virginia Congressman Don Beyer fired a longtime aide after it emerged that she was scheduling meetings with congressional staffers on behalf of the Chinese embassy.

But while these serious scandals received extensive media coverage, a more insidious and subversive scandal has festered for decades with less attention. That scandal is the rise of what I call the New China Lobby.

The original China Lobby was a coalition of patriotic American anti-Communists who supported Chiang Kai-shek and his Nationalist Party in Taiwan. The China Lobby urged Washington policymakers to provide military aid to Chiang and righteously opposed American or foreign diplomatic recognition of the mainland Chinese Communists. Remarkably, this old China Lobby delayed the United Nations' recognition of Mao's government for more than twenty years and steeled American resolve to defend Taiwan from Communist conquest.

But the tide turned with Richard Nixon's opening to China in 1972, which fostered the rise of a New China Lobby. A mirror image of the original China Lobby, this one championed engagement with China and a turn from Taiwan. Nixon, Secretary of State Henry Kissinger, and an unlikely alliance of influential liberals, diplomats, and public intellectuals brought this new pro-China approach into the Washington mainstream as a supposed way to counter Soviet Russia.

The New China Lobby helped secure America's formal diplomatic recognition for China in 1979 and never looked back. Most-favored-nation trade status soon followed. The Carter and Reagan administrations provided military equipment to Beijing. In 1989, the Bush administration meekly reacted to China's mass slaughter of its own people in Tiananmen Square. Just days after the Tiananmen Square Massacre, Kissinger urged the United States not to apply sanctions and wrote that "the drama in Beijing" is "a test of our political maturity."

Yet far from fading away when the Cold War ended in 1991—its supposed rationale—the New China Lobby grew even stronger. It would be as if the United States had renewed the vows of its marriage of convenience with Soviet Russia in 1945 after we defeated Nazi Germany together—worse, actually, given that we worked much more closely with Russia in World War II than we ever did with China in the Cold War.

But given a taste of the China market after 1979, corporate America by the 1990s was hooked. The New China Lobby pressured Congress, bankrolled campaigns of politicians sympathetic to China, and amplified pro-

China voices. After cowing Bill Clinton into backing off his campaign promise to tie preferential trade status to China's human-rights record, the *Washington Post* dubbed American business "the backbone of the new China lobby." Even back then, the *Post* noted how China kept its lobby in line: "For every carrot it hands out, Beijing shakes the stick. U.S. companies are regularly threatened with cancellation of orders or loss of future deals if China loses its preferred [trade] status."

Thanks to these efforts of the New China Lobby, China gained permanent most-favored-nation status in 2000 and entry into the World Trade Organization the following year. As we saw in chapter 3, these foolish decisions supercharged China's economic conquest, and the New China Lobby's vested interests in China. In the previous chapter, we saw some examples of the lobby at work—whether it was Wall Street bankers supporting China's trade negotiators or corporate giants lobbying for Chinese slave labor. But when so much money is at stake, it goes much further than that.

For one, Chinese companies and entities directly hire Washington power brokers to advocate for their interests on Capitol Hill. Former Senate Majority Leader Trent Lott, for example, along with prominent former Senator John Breaux lobbied on behalf of TikTok, the social-media giant owned by the Chinese company ByteDance. So did dozens of former high-ranking congressional aides, including aides to former House Speaker Paul

Ryan and former Senate Majority Leaders Harry Reid and Bill Frist. The money TikTok and its parent threw around Washington was obscene. One longtime lobbyist told me that TikTok offered him $100,000 per month, which he declined because of the company's contribution to antisemitism after Hamas's October 7 atrocity against Israel.

Other examples abound. Former Senators David Vitter and Barbara Boxer both lobbied for a Chinese company that provided facial-recognition technology and hundreds of millions of dollars in services to Xinjiang's genocidal authorities. Former House Foreign Affairs Committee chair Ed Royce lobbied for Tencent, the tech giant that helped censor the NBA. Former Senator Joe Lieberman lobbied for the blacklisted Chinese telecom giant ZTE, which he had criticized as a security risk while in public office.

But it's not only former lawmakers and officials working for China after they leave office; the revolving door goes both ways. China's sympathizers and advocates too often return to office and bring their pro-China instincts with them. Take, for instance, every modern secretary of the Treasury. Coming mostly from Wall Street, they have tended to have a strong affinity for China, if not deep ties to it.

And sometimes it's more explicit. In 2021, President Biden nominated Christopher Fonzone, who had represented the Chinese telecom giant Huawei, as the intelligence community's top lawyer. Fonzone had previously served on President Obama's National Security Council, so he knew well the dangers Huawei posed to America. What's more, he refused to foreclose working for companies like Huawei in the future. I opposed Fonzone's nomination and delivered a simple warning to members of the New China Lobby on the Senate floor. "If you wish to serve in the United States government in the future, let me be very clear," I warned. "Do not do business with the Chinese Communist Party, or its military, or the companies that support it. Stop it today. Don't take the work. Don't take the meeting. Don't cash the check." I opposed the nomination of Kate Heinzelman as the CIA's top lawyer on the same grounds: she had worked for a Chinese pharmaceutical giant and refused to rule out similar work in the future.

One other technique of the Chinese Communists is to target the family members of politicians and officials. Of course, the most egregious and notorious example is Hunter Biden. He earned more than half his total income from Chinese businesses between 2013 and 2018, rode on Air Force Two with his father to business meetings in Beijing, and helped arrange White House meetings for Chinese clients. Hunter knew full well what he was doing: he and his uncle Jim (Joe Biden's brother) even met with a Chinese associate whom Hunter called the "spy chief of China." What's most concerning about the Hunter Biden saga is the credible evidence that Joe Biden personally assisted his son's efforts to curry favor with the Chinese Communists while also benefiting from the riches paid to his family.

Although the Hunter Biden story is the most extreme, it's not unique. China also cultivated, for instance, members of the Bush family. Prescott Bush Jr. started doing business in China in the 1980s, when his brother was vice president, and he was among the first American businessmen to return to China after the Tiananmen Square Massacre. After his brother lost the presidency, he helped form a pro-China lobbying group known as the U.S.–China Chamber of Commerce. He acknowledged that his family ties were a "big asset" in China and advised other businessmen "to be sure you've got the party bosses working with you."

Neil Bush followed a similar path when his brother became president in 2001. He has traveled to China more than 150 times, raking in millions of dollars and aiding the Chinese regime and its companies. He received over $2 million from a Chinese semiconductor firm partly led by Jiang Zemin's son, served on the board of a Chinese company that illegally provided $1.3 million to his brother Jeb's 2016 campaign, and even sent two million respiratory masks from North America to China at the start of the coronavirus pandemic. In 2019, Neil delivered a speech condemning criticism of China's human-rights record, surveillance state, and Thousand

Talents plan as "clearly flawed and based on half-truths or all-out fake news."

Although there's no evidence that either President Bush was influenced by his respective brother's business dealings, it's nonetheless telling how widely China casts its net. And that approach extends to state and local governments.

Espionage Closer to Home

Former Speaker of the House Thomas "Tip" O'Neil famously remarked that "all politics is local." The Chinese Communist Party has taken this maxim to heart. While one might think China cares mostly about, say, trade and defense policy with our federal government and little about what happens in your state and hometown, that very complacency helps the party infiltrate our local and state governments, using these footholds of influence to pressure Washington politicians to extract economic concessions.

China has several reasons to cultivate strong ties with local and state politicians. These elected officials are something of a farm team for Congress. Today's mayor, city councillor, state legislator, or governor may be tomorrow's congressman, senator, or cabinet secretary. And not only that: most presidents in my lifetime got their start in local and state government. China builds relationships with these politicians as a way of collecting potential future national leaders. Meanwhile, it can use these local and state officials as de facto lobbyists to their congressional delegations. Also, these officials can offer Chinese companies concrete economic benefits like subsidies, tax breaks, and land grants.

For their part, most state and local politicians of course don't sympathize with the Chinese Communist Party, but rather see China as a source of investment and jobs for their states and cities. Nothing wrong with that in principle: many local economies need a lot of help. But Chinese money isn't a Japanese car company or a German manufacturer looking for the best deal to build a plant in the United States. Chinese Communists understand these economic and political incentives and leverage them to the hilt, which too many politicians either don't appreciate or actively ignore.

We've already encountered a prime example of China's start-early strategy for rising politicians. Christine Fang, the Chinese spy acting covertly as a Democratic activist and fundraiser, initiated her relationship with Eric Swalwell, an ambitious politician who was on the move from an early age, when he was a young city councilman. Within just a few years, he was a congressman sitting on the House Intelligence Committee. But he wasn't Fang's only target. She also cultivated a relationship with Fremont Mayor Bill Harrison, traveled the country attending mayoral conferences, and reportedly had affairs with as many as fifteen mayors.

A less salacious though still insidious technique to develop relationships with local officials is the so-called sister-city program, which pairs our local governments with those in foreign countries to promote business ties and cultural exchanges—laudable goals when the sister cities are in, say, Finland or Japan. But China, predictably, has weaponized its more than 150 sister-city relationships in the United States. Chinese Communists wine and dine often-unsuspecting American mayors and other local officials, even providing free travel for them to visit their Chinese sister cities. Chinese officials then deluge these officials with Communist propaganda and promises of lots of jobs and business opportunities back home. In exchange, the Communists often ask these American officials to lobby their congressmen and senators to go easy on China and to introduce them to local American business leaders. Sometimes Chinese officials require their American counterparts to recognize that Taiwan is part of China as a condition of the relationship.

These sister-city relationships can be minimal or extensive, depending on how gullible or desperate the targeted local officials are. San Francisco, for example, started its sister-city relationship with Shanghai in 1980, but it deepened considerably under Mayor Gavin Newsom. In 2008, the torch for what critics labeled the "Genocide Olympics" stopped in San Francisco on its way to Beijing. Human-rights activists lined the torch-bearer's declared route to highlight China's crimes in Tibet and its support of Sudan's genocidal regime. But at the last moment, Newsom changed the route, turning the event into what the *New York Times* called "an elaborate game of hide-and-seek." Newsom claimed that he changed the route for security concerns, but the president of his board of supervisors said, "He did it so China can report they had a great torch run." That same year, Newsom forged an economic-development initiative with China that it used to attract investment and propel its green-energy sector. The city even hosted speed dating events with Chinese companies soliciting American investments. One company admitted that it wanted to be known as a "U.S. company that does its manufacturing in China."

China forged a similarly strong partnership with Detroit's Mayor Michael Duggan and Michigan Governor Rick Snyder. Snyder traveled to China eight times and even created a state "Michigan/China Week." Duggan said that Detroit's relationship with its sister city Chongqing and with China generally was "a high priority," and he even tried to form a second Chinese sister-city relationship. China used the relationship with Duggan not only to influence powerful politicians in a critical swing state, but also to advance its own automobile industry. Chinese officials and businessmen repeatedly met with the Motor City's best experts and forged research partnerships with the state. Rising tensions with China haven't changed their views, either. In 2023, Duggan said he was "very anxious" to rebuild relations with China, and Snyder's successor, Gretchen Whitmer, welcomed a controversial joint venture between Ford and a Chinese electric-battery maker to Michigan. Through the new battery factory, the Chinese company will directly benefit from both federal and state subsidies—your tax dollars at work.

Barack Obama's hometown of Chicago has not one but two sister cities in China, Shanghai and Shenyang. Mayor Richard Daley's long-standing cultivation of the Chinese Communist Party paid big dividends in 2011, when China's then general secretary, Hu Jintao, traveled to Chicago during a state visit. Daley declared that Chicago was "the most China-friendly city in the United States" and said he wanted to make it "China's economic 'Gateway to America.'" He unironically toasted the wooden and uninspiring Hu as a "man of vision" and promised that "we have a strong commitment to building friendship and economic ties into not only government but the business community." Hu and Daley also visited a high-school Confucius Institute, celebrating the party's infiltration of American education—at the time, Chicago was home to the world's largest Confucius Institute. Perhaps unsurprisingly, Daley directly profited from his China connections after leaving office a few months later, and Communist officials even gave him the honorary title of "Special Adviser to the Municipality of Wuhan." No word on whether lab safety was part of his honorary duties.

Chinese officials don't always play so nice with their American counterparts. New York City has had a sister-city relationship with Beijing since 1979. In 2023, the Chinese consulate there threatened Mayor Eric Adams against attending a banquet honoring the Taiwanese president; Adams obeyed and skipped out. (Such threats aren't unusual: China has threatened me about past trips to Taiwan, which I of course still took.) But some mayors are made of tougher stuff. In 2024, a Chinese diplomat warned the mayor of Belleville, New Jersey—a township of not even forty thousand residents—not to raise a Tibetan flag at a local event. Fortunately, the mayor of little Belleville had more backbone than the mayor of New York and raised the flag anyway.

Beyond mayors and city officials, there's no more tempting or valuable target in our states than our nation's governors. This threat is so acute but so often overlooked that Secretary of State Mike Pompeo warned about it at the National Governors Association conference in 2020. He told the assembled governors that Chinese Communists monitor their activities. In fact, Pompeo explained, "they've labeled each of you friendly, hardline, or ambiguous. I'll let you decide where you think you belong. Someone in China already has. Many of you, indeed, in the report are referenced by name." Later that year, Pompeo also revoked American participation in the U.S.-China Governors Forum to Promote Sub-National Cooperation because China used it to "directly and malignly influence state and local leaders."

One person who didn't take the warning to heart was Gavin Newsom, China's old friend, who had graduated from mayor to governor—another example, by the way, of China's start-early strategy. In 2023, Newsom became the first governor to visit China in more than four years. During the visit, he invoked a lot of conciliatory platitudes like "divorce is not an option" and "we are better when we are cooperating and competing, not cold shouldering one another." The Chinese Communists got their desired photo op, and Newsom got, well, his desired photo op—because he certainly got nothing else of value in return. Newsom admitted that he didn't raise the issues of China's crimes in Tibet, Xinjiang, and Hong Kong during his meeting with Xi Jinping, the Chinese dictator, but he swore—maybe he even pinky-promised—that he raised the issues with China's foreign minister in private.

The next month, Newsom returned the favor. He welcomed Xi to an international summit in San Francisco, whose streets were miraculously free of human waste. I guess Newsom can clean up his city for a Communist dictator, but not for his own people. He also feted Xi as the guest of honor at a ritzy banquet with business leaders like Tim Cook and Larry Fink, who of course gave the Communist dictator a standing ovation.

My own state isn't immune to Chinese overtures. Arkansas Governor Mike Beebe traveled to China in 2012 and met with several unnamed companies, noting one especially promising prospect for South Arkansas's timber industry. When Governor Asa Hutchinson took office in 2015, he took this baton and ran even harder after Chinese investment, making three trips to China in his first three years in office. He and his chief of staff also spoke and met regularly with officials from the Chinese consulate in Houston. And it didn't help matters that Hutchinson's son traveled with the governor to China while representing Chinese clients, including at least three Chinese companies that received millions of dollars in subsidies from Hutchinson's administration.

By 2017, Hutchinson was touting $1.4 billion in promised Chinese investment. The crown jewel was a massive paper mill by the Chinese company Sun Paper in South Arkansas, which he called "one of the largest private investments in the history of the state of Arkansas." Strangely enough, though, the Chinese kept delaying construction, sweetening the deal with promises of even more investment, and then delaying again. Their favorite excuse was Donald Trump's "trade war," even though the president had provided specific exemptions for the company.

Watching from afar, I concluded that China was using these proposed investments, especially the Sun Paper mill, to leverage state officials against the Trump administration and our congressional delegation—including me. Within a year of the Sun Paper "deal," Hutchinson began encouraging me to meet with the Chinese consul general from Houston in Arkansas. I politely deflected at first, but he kept at it. Finally, I answered that I spend my time in Arkansas meeting with Arkansans (not Communists, I should've added), and if the Chinese really wanted to meet, the ambassador could come to my Washington office. Hutchinson objected, explaining that the Houston consulate managed Chinese investment in our state. I replied that I definitely wouldn't meet the consul general in that case, because I didn't want the Chinese Communists to suspect that I'd pull my punches for a mess of pottage for our state. A dumbfounded Hutchinson was speechless.

In 2020, inevitably, Sun Paper scrapped its planned investment in Arkansas. That same year, not coincidentally, the Trump administration shut down China's Houston consulate because it was, as Pompeo put it, a "den of spies." Thick, billowing smoke was seen rising out of the consulate as those spies raced to burn sensitive documents, perhaps including its plans to influence Arkansas politics.

I don't believe these politicians are witting accomplices of the Chinese Communist Party; on the contrary, most are acting with good intentions to improve often troubled local economies. But the party manipulated their good intentions for its own purposes, as it has done with so many Americans from so many walks of life.

We've now seen how Chinese Communists have targeted our businesses, our media, our universities, and our government. But perhaps worst of all, they're targeting our future: Chinese Communists are coming for our kids.

VI.

China Is Coming for Our Kids

The Chinese Communist Party has secured a foothold across most major institutions in our country, but the party isn't content with today—it also wants to influence our future, namely, our children. China has targeted our kids through their smartphones and wants to corrupt what they learn in our schools. Worst of all, China has manufactured the deadliest drug crisis in American history, killing and maiming thousands of teenagers every year.

Put simply, our kids have become some of the earliest casualties in China's Cold War against America.

TikTok

No social-media app has harmed our kids more than TikTok. If your kid uses TikTok, I urge you to stop reading now and immediately delete the account. Then you can read on about how this Chinese platform addicts our kids, harvests their data, promotes harmful content and behaviors, and spreads Chinese Communist propaganda.

Despite TikTok's protests, there's no doubt the Chinese Communist Party controls this social-media platform. TikTok's parent company, technology giant ByteDance, is headquartered in China. As with all technology companies in China, the party strictly monitors and censors ByteDance, requires it to surrender any data upon request, and embeds a party cell inside the company. One former ByteDance executive revealed that this cell can access all company data through a "superuser" credential. The Chinese government also uses its "golden share" of ByteDance stock to gain a seat on the board of directors and influence the company.

Speaking of that golden share, ByteDance appointed a Singaporean named Shou Chew to be TikTok's CEO the day after the government acquired it. Chew is best known in America for his disgraceful testimony before Congress during which, for instance, he refused to answer whether TikTok spied on Americans or to acknowledge the genocide in Xinjiang. When I asked him about the curious timing of his promotion, he claimed it was just a "coincidence"—some coincidence! In reality, Chew had served as ByteDance's chief financial officer, lived in Beijing for at least five years, and had worked for a blacklisted Chinese company doing business with the People's Liberation Army. The Chinese Communist

Party knew exactly what they were getting with Chew at TikTok.

In a terrible mistake, we allowed this Communist-controlled app into our country. More than 150 million Americans have downloaded the app—especially kids. By 2023, more than 60 percent of American teenagers used TikTok, spending an average of ninety minutes a day on the app. But TikTok really uses them. Its highly sophisticated algorithm analyzes their every move to discern their tastes, hopes, and fears and harvests sensitive information like their mental health. As a result, one in five teenage girls and more than one in ten teenage boys report using the app "almost constantly," more than any other major social-media app.

While TikTok is far from the only social-media platform to use manipulative algorithms, the key difference is Chinese Communist control, which creates unique risks to our kids' privacy, mental health, and exposure to Communist propaganda. Though most users may tend to watch silly cat tricks, fun dance videos, cooking recipes, and so forth, there's something a lot more sinister going on underneath the hood. Let's take a look.

First, TikTok hoovers up massive amounts of data about our kids: their names, ages, email accounts, addresses, phone numbers, credit-card numbers, facial features, voiceprints, keystrokes, direct messages, photos, videos, and viewing habits. Chew testified that TikTok doesn't share data with ByteDance, but that was yet another lie. In 2024, a former senior data scientist for TikTok confessed to attending regular meetings with ByteDance executives and to sending Americans' data to ByteDance every two weeks. And that's just one whistle-blower. The Chinese Communist Party has that data forever and can use it against our children for the rest of their lives.

Second, TikTok purposely targets manipulative, obscene, and dangerous materials at our kids. Several studies and lawsuits have revealed that within minutes of a teenager's downloading the app—and that's before the user expresses preferences or views many videos— TikTok recommends content related to pornography, eating disorders, and suicide. For example, a *Wall Street Journal* investigation created an account pretending to be a thirteen-year-old, and TikTok bombarded it with nearly six hundred videos about drug use. TikTok inundated 90 percent of another "teenager's" video feed with explicit sexual material.

The consequences of TikTok's manipulative algorithm can be severe. In 2020, a fourteen-year-old girl got addicted to weight-loss and eating-disorder videos on TikTok. After only a few months on the app, she had purged 20 percent of her body weight, her hair was falling out, and her mom had to seek medical treatment to put her on a feeding tube. TikTok has promoted a "Corpse Bride Diet" so severe that it could leave a girl's bones easily visible through her skin. In 2022, a fifteen-year-old girl told the *Wall Street Journal* that she tried to block eating-disorder content on TikTok, but "I still see posts related to eating disorders on my feed at least three times a day."

It gets worse. TikTok poses a lethal threat to the one in four American teenagers who seriously consider suicide. In 2022, TikTok drove sixteen-year-old Chase Nasca to take his own life. His mother discovered that he had searched the app for motivational speeches, but TikTok instead fed him horrific material encouraging suicide, including a video of an oncoming train that was darkly captioned, "went for a quick lil walk to clear my head." Five days later, Nasca stood on a notoriously dangerous stretch of railroad tracks near his home and was run over by a train.

That same year, a sixteen-year-old Arkansan named Mason Edens was deeply depressed after a breakup and turned to TikTok. Edens also searched for motivational content, including "positive affirmations" and "inspirational quotes," but instead TikTok served up content encouraging him to take his own life. Some videos encouraged suicide to "prove your love to your soulmate." Another video, which Edens liked, stated that "I wanna put a shotgun to my f—— mouth and blow my brains out." At least four other videos recommended a similar method of suicide. Edens ultimately shot and killed himself. His heartbroken mother told NBC News, "I completely believe in my heart that Mason would be alive today had he not seen those TikTok videos."

By contrast, the Chinese version of TikTok encourages Chinese teenagers, in effect, to eat their vegetables, do their homework, and respect their elders—and it's available to them for only forty minutes at night. In fact, isn't it telling that ByteDance doesn't offer TikTok inside China?

Third, TikTok also promotes the interests of the Chinese Communist Party, which is especially worrisome because so many young Americans rely on TikTok for news. In 2023, one third of Americans aged eighteen to twenty-nine regularly got their news from TikTok, a fourfold increase from 2020. There's less data on the news habits of American teens, but a study from Great Britain found that TikTok is the top news source for British kids ages twelve to fifteen. The same is almost certainly true for our kids.

China exploits this information pipeline to America's youth to spread Communist propaganda and censor negative content. Compared to Instagram, for example, TikTok featured fewer than 10 percent of hashtags on the Uyghur genocide, fewer than 7 percent on Taiwan, fewer than 5 percent on the South China Sea, fewer than 3 percent related to Tibet, and fewer than 1 percent on Hong Kong and Tiananmen Square. In 2019, TikTok even suspended a New Jersey teenager's account for posting a video critical of China's genocide in Xinjiang. And during the pandemic, TikTok outright banned the term "China Virus."

Likewise, TikTok amplifies content that harms the interests of China's opponents. For example, TikTok had nearly 230 million posts with some variation of #StandwithKashmir, a separatist movement in India, compared to fewer than 400,000 Instagram posts with that hashtag, a ratio of more than 600 to 1. And in weeks after the October 7 atrocity by Hamas against Israel, TikTok had 210,000 posts with the hashtag #StandwithPalestine, compared to only 17,000 posts with #StandwithIsrael. The app also suppresses pro-Ukraine content and content critical of China's Iranian allies.

TikTok is such a dangerous spy app that it produced a rare large bipartisan vote in Congress in April 2024 to force ByteDance to divest from the app to keep it operating in the United States. Indeed, during the congressional debate, TikTok revealed how it could be used to influence American politics by sending push notices to its users' smartphones, asking them to contact their representatives to lobby against the bill. Some kids even called congressional offices and threatened to kill themselves if the bill passed. Just imagine what TikTok might do, for instance, during a conflict between China and Taiwan. As of this writing, TikTok has sued to overturn the law, and ByteDance, under Chinese government direction, has refused to sell the app—a telling sign of TikTok's importance to the plans of the Chinese Communist Party.

Whatever the fate of TikTok, though, it's not the only way China seeks to influence our kids. China is also infiltrating our schools.

Chinese Communist Schoolmasters

The Chinese Communist Party has spent millions of dollars to influence what our kids learn, who teaches them, and who learns alongside them. Since at least 2009, China has dispensed grants, established miniature Confucius Institutes, deployed teachers, shaped curriculum, and provided books and other materials to American schools. China has also sent thousands of students to our schools and has even outright bought some American schools. Put simply, Chinese Communists are very keen on influencing what our children learn about their evil empire.

China has used Confucius Institutes not only as a beachhead on college campuses, but also to extend Chinese influence into our primary and secondary schools. These institutes have led the way in establishing Chinese language and cultural programs, called "Confucius Classrooms," in more than five hundred schools—most often at America's best grade schools. The University of Maryland Confucius Institute, for example, helped create ten affiliated Confucius Classrooms throughout Maryland.

Though school principals and vice principals ostensibly managed the Confucius Classrooms program, in reality, the Confucius Institutes shaped everything, from work plan to budgets, while also arranging for Chinese nationals to enter the United States to teach. And the Confucius Institutes took direction from the Chinese Hanban, China's government agency overseeing the institutes.

Confucius Classrooms were a longtime Hanban priority. One Hanban official wrote to the U.S. director of Confucius Institutes that these classrooms "will be very rewarding for our efforts." Li Changchun, a former chief of Communist propaganda, admitted that the institutes "are an important part of China's overseas propaganda setup." He later added that by "using the excuse of teaching Chinese language, everything looks reasonable and logical." But propaganda was always the goal. For example, the director general of the Confucius Institute headquarters crowed that "every mainland teacher we send . . . will say Taiwan belongs to China. We should have one China. No hesitation." Likewise, the Hanban website claimed that the United States had forced China into the Korean War by bombing Chinese villages—which, of course, is a lie—and called Taiwan "China's largest island." None of this was a secret, yet a Chinese government agency was allowed to partner with American schools and approve teachers for our kids.

China especially wants to shape what our children

learn about the Chinese language and Chinese history. Parents Defending Education, an advocacy group opposed to politicized agendas in the classroom, has traced nearly $18 million in grants from China to 143 school districts. These grants paid in part for American teachers to attend Confucius Institute conferences and even to travel to China to learn how to teach our kids. Other grants paid for Chinese instructors to teach American students directly.

China has also partnered with the College Board to indoctrinate our children. You may know the College Board as the organization that oversees the SAT and designs Advanced Placement courses for American high schools, but it also works closely with the Hanban. So closely, in fact, that College Board CEO David Coleman gushed in 2014 that "Hanban is just like the sun. It lights the path to develop Chinese teaching in the U.S. The College Board is the moon. I am so honored to reflect the light that we've gotten from Hanban."

One example of the College Board reflecting Hanban's light was an ill-conceived guest-teacher program. Between 2007 and 2020, the Hanban sent 1,650 Chinese teachers to the United States as a part of this program. These teachers came here with a purpose. Dan Currell and Mick Zais, former Department of Education officials, explain that these "teachers are trained to steer classroom discussions away from an ever-expanding list of issues:

Taiwan, Tibet, Tiananmen Square, Hong Kong, Xinjiang, Inner Mongolia, the South China Sea, and more. The problem isn't what is being said in Confucius lessons; the problem is what is not being said." The teachers' objective is to "normalize" the Chinese Communist Party.

The College Board also coordinates with China to shape curriculum in our schools. The Chinese government paid the College Board $685,000 to help design the Advanced Placement Chinese language test, furtively influencing the curriculum at schools across our country. According to the National Association of Scholars, Chinese influence may be one reason American students learn a simplified version of the Chinese language, popularized by Mao. As a result, most American students can't read pre-Communist Chinese literature or Taiwanese or Hong Kong texts.

The College Board claims that it no longer accepts grants from Hanban—which it announced only after fellow senators and I pressed it. But it hasn't cleansed China's influence from its curriculum or regretted its past collaboration with Chinese Communists, a typical response when a venerable American institution gets caught in bed with China.

And China doesn't work only through intermediaries like the Confucius Institutes and the College Board; it also infiltrates our schools directly. In 2018 alone, America's schools enrolled 42,000 Chinese nationals. While that number had fallen to around 14,000 by 2022, Chinese students remain the largest foreign-student population in our schools. As with the Confucius Classrooms, these students often gravitate to America's elite schools. The presence of these students—typically the children of powerful and well-connected Chinese parents—doubtless influences how some of our top schools discuss China and its Communist government. And when these students enroll at private school, paying full-freight tuition, they inevitably add to the New China Lobby, with the headmaster, the school board, and local politicians having a strong financial incentive to encourage their representatives and senators to take it easy on China.

Sometimes, though, Chinese parents don't merely enroll their kids at private schools—they buy the school outright. In 2017, for example, a Chinese firm spent half a billion dollars to buy a network of private schools in California. Another Chinese company owns more than two hundred private schools across the country, including one of America's best prep schools, in Brooklyn, New York. Chinese entities can even buy American military academies. For example, a senior Chinese Communist purchased New York Military Academy, Donald Trump's alma mater, and then appointed several of his Chinese associates to its board of trustees. Yet the Department of Defense has granted this academy hundreds of thousands of dollars since its Chinese takeover.

China's manipulation of our kids through their smartphones and schools is bad enough, but the Chinese Communists aren't satisfied with simply manipulating or influencing them. China is also poisoning and killing our kids.

The Reverse Opium War

The Chinese Communists aren't only mass murderers, invaders, and liars—they're also drug dealers. The Chinese Communist Party has unleashed the deadliest drug crisis in our history by engineering and fueling the fentanyl epidemic that's devastating America's youth.

China's central role in the fentanyl epidemic is rather ironic, given how Chinese Communists still lecture Westerners about the Opium Wars. In the early nineteenth century, European nations exported large amounts of opium into China, causing widespread addiction and destabilizing Chinese society. In 1839, Chinese imperial authorities cracked down, burning imported British opium, executing Chinese merchants, and threatening foreign sellers. The ensuing First Opium War ended with a decisive British victory, and the subsequent Second Opium War ended with an equally lopsided British and French victory. A series of tough treaties forced China to cede territory, pay reparations, and permit the opium trade, among other concessions. These wars and treaties started what Chinese Communists call "the century of humiliation" that ended only with China's emergence from World War II and Mao's victory in the Chinese Civil War. Chinese leaders still complain about these events today, as if American teenagers were responsible for what Europeans did nearly two centuries ago.

In fact, when it comes to dealing drugs, the Chinese Communist Party has plenty to answer for, going back to the Chinese Civil War. In 1945, more than 40 percent of Communist revenues came from selling opium to fellow Chinese. According to historians Jung Chang and Jon Halliday, Mao trumpeted his drug dealing in private as "the Revolutionary Opium War."

And here's yet another case where Chinese Communists have continued Mao's toxic legacy. The bipartisan House Select Committee on the Chinese Communist Party found that China provides 80 percent of methamphetamine precursors used by cartels in Mexico, exports ketamine throughout Southeast Asia, and smuggles opioids into India and Africa.

But its worst drug crime is the mass production and sale of fentanyl and its precursor ingredients into North America. Virtually all the fentanyl sold on American streets today comes either from China or from Mexico, where it's made with Chinese-supplied ingredients and tools.

America has never battled a drug like fentanyl, which is fifty times stronger than heroin. Just two milligrams—

roughly equivalent to a few grains of sand—can kill you. Fentanyl has fueled the worst drug epidemic in our nation's history, with more than one hundred thousand Americans now dying from drug overdoses on average in each of the last few years—nearly double the number of American deaths during the entire Vietnam War. And it's getting worse: more Americans died from fentanyl alone in 2021 than died from every drug combined in 2017. When it doesn't kill, fentanyl maims, cripples, and addicts millions more Americans and feeds the worst homelessness crisis on record.

The fentanyl crisis hits young Americans especially hard. Fentanyl is now the leading cause of death for Americans aged eighteen to forty-five, and it kills more Americans aged fifteen to nineteen than any natural cause. Between 2019 and 2021, fentanyl was responsible for 84 percent of all adolescent overdose deaths, and by 2022 nearly two dozen high-school-age kids were dying from drug overdoses every week. Kids sometimes don't even know they're taking fentanyl because the Chinese drug is often spliced into nearly every other drug, from heroin and cocaine to Adderall and marijuana.

This drug crisis didn't just happen—the Chinese Communist Party purposely designed it. Chinese chemists and criminals have sold fentanyl and its precursor ingredients for years into North America with the full knowledge and even direct support of the Chinese government. The House Select Committee on the Chinese

Communist Party concluded that China provides direct subsidies, rebates, grants, and awards for companies producing fentanyl and fentanyl precursors sold into America. According to internal documents, some of these companies even boast about tax exemptions for their poisonous products. In other cases, the Chinese government directly owns these companies or holds a "golden share" of stock to influence a company through its board of directors, as it does with TikTok.

China's government also shields its fentanyl peddlers from legal consequences for their crimes. For instance, China refuses to extradite or prosecute fentanyl manufacturers and tips them off about foreign investigations. Even when China acknowledges that these merchants of death have broken Chinese law, it refuses to prosecute them. In 2022, China's foreign minister admitted that "not a single criminal case has been opened in China that involves the manufacturing, trafficking and smuggling of fentanyl-related substances." And while it blocks drug-smuggling websites for its own subjects, the Chinese government allows its companies to advertise sales of fentanyl and its precursors to foreigners with impunity.

As usual, China has repeatedly broken its promises to end this drug warfare. Xi Jinping made deals with Presidents Obama, Trump, and Biden to crack down on fentanyl trafficking. But more Americans continued to die from fentanyl after each empty promise. Only President Trump secured a major concession when Xi agreed to schedule fentanyl as a controlled substance. Yet the Chinese dictator made no such promise about the chemical precursors for fentanyl. Chinese producers thus shifted from smuggling fentanyl into the United States to sending fentanyl precursors to Mexico, where drug cartels manufacture the drug in massive quantities. China even provides pill presses to the cartels and assists them with financing and money laundering. Our former commanding general for Latin America has testified that Chinese money launderers are now the "number one underwriter" of drug trafficking in the Western Hemisphere.

The epidemic may not stop with fentanyl, either. Chinese drug traffickers are helping produce new, more potent drugs—some of them twenty-five times stronger than fentanyl, so strong that Narcan can't reverse an overdose. The high from one such drug is so extreme that users exhibit a shuffling, incoherent, zombie-like stupor; some of these drugs even rot addicts' flesh.

A Chinese official who led the crackdown on opium before the Opium Wars wrote to Queen Victoria, "Let us ask, where is your conscience?" The same question could be asked today of Xi Jinping, but we know the answer. A man who commits genocide against his own people won't hesitate to commit any depravity against foreign adversaries, very much including the poisoning of children.

China is waging a Reverse Opium War against America—or perhaps a second Revolutionary Opium War.

The ravages are stark and severe: the Chinese Communist Party is a leading cause of death for young Americans.

* * *

The Chinese Communists have crossed every line of decency, committed every sin imaginable, and are waging war on our children, our families, and our nation. Yet, they've mostly gotten away it, making obscene profits and extending their influence around the world. Indeed, they're still toasted by our billionaires, accommodated by our politicians, and praised by our elites.

This lamentable reality brings us to perhaps the most unsayable truth of all: China could win.

VII.

||||||||||||||||||||||||||||||||||||||||||

China Could Win

No living American knows what it's like to live in a world where another nation calls the shots. Most of us take American global dominance for granted, without thinking much about it; since at least World War I, that's just the way it's been. World trade is conducted in dollars. English is the unofficial global language of business and politics. When there's a crisis somewhere in the world, nations look to America first. Most world leaders have to regularly ask themselves: How will the Americans react? For more than a century, Americans have reaped enormous economic and security benefits from this state of affairs.

The Chinese Communist Party wants to overturn this status quo. Bill Rood, a legendary teacher of international relations, liked to say that "you run the show or the show runs you." The Chinese Communists are tired of letting America run the show. That's why they've accumulated so much military, economic, and technological power and so thoroughly infiltrated American society and government. They want to supplant us as the world's dominant superpower.

There's one key piece of the puzzle for China: Taiwan. The Chinese Communist Party knows that without Taiwan it cannot win the struggle with America for global supremacy; whereas with Taiwan, victory would be attainable.

When I speak about China and Taiwan, I'm sometimes asked why Taiwan matters so much. That's a reasonable question. After all, it's a small island on the other side of the world, barely one hundred miles off China's coast. Moreover, as horrific and infamous as are China's crimes against Tibet, Xinjiang, and Hong Kong, those haven't led to a global depression, the fraying of U.S. military alliances, nuclear proliferation, the decline of American influence, long-term economic stagnation, or the sun finally setting on American power.

But Taiwan is different, and its fall could lead to all that and more. China itself tells us so, not only with its rhetoric, but also with its actions. As we saw in chapter 2, China's breakneck military buildup aims above all at the rapid invasion and occupation of Taiwan. Nations don't undertake such massive and risky projects unless they mean it—and they mean it only when the stakes are the highest imaginable. Let's look, then, at the natural and logical consequences of a war over Taiwan and what they mean for America's future.

For most Americans, the immediate effect of China's invasion of Taiwan would be economic chaos. According to Bloomberg Economics, a war in Taiwan would wipe out $10 trillion in wealth worldwide. The American economy would shrink by much more than it did in the Great Recession of 2008. No one today has lived through such an economic collapse. Ian Easton, a U.S. Naval War College professor and expert on China's planned Taiwan invasion, writes, "It is possible that a Chinese invasion of Taiwan would cause a 21st century version of the Great Depression." Famed investor Ken Griffin is blunter: "It's an immediate Great Depression."

The pain and hardship would be severe for all Americans. An inevitable stock-market crash would erase the life savings of millions of Americans. Many millions more would lose their jobs as unemployment spiked. The abrupt severing of economic ties with China would also lead to shortages, empty shelves, and soaring prices at stores like Walmart, Costco, and Target. China would likely make good on its threat during the pandemic to cut off our supply of critical medicines and medical equipment, with deadly consequences.

This economic catastrophe would result in no small part from Taiwan's unique role in the global semiconductor industry. Taiwan manufactures around 60 percent of the world's semiconductors and 90 percent of the world's most advanced semiconductors. These microchips power everything from automobiles to smartphones to kitchen appliances, accounting for trillions of dollars in global economic value. Any war, regardless of the outcome, would immediately disrupt these supply chains and likely destroy most of the chip factories. If you tried to buy a car in 2022 or 2023, you probably recall low inventories and high prices. That experience is just a small foretaste of what a war in Taiwan would bring.

There's no happy ending, either, whatever happens in the war. These chips aren't commodities like oil, which can be replaced with supply from elsewhere. China would struggle to rebuild factories of similar quality; so would the United States, as halting efforts to build cutting-edge chip factories at home have demonstrated. Even if China somehow seized the island without destroying the factories, that would give the Chinese Communists a total stranglehold on one of the world's most vital commercial products.

No American industry would escape unscathed. Our automobile industry and all its supporting industries—steel, aluminum, spare parts, dealerships, and so forth—would be devastated. Silicon Valley and the entire technology sector would come to a near standstill; for years, Americans might be unable to buy new computers, smartphones, or other everyday electronics. Every other industry that depends on automobiles and technology—which is to say, all of them, from transportation to agriculture to energy—would suffer as well.

Of course, a global depression would also hit China

hard, and one might ask why the Chinese Communist Party would cut off its nose to spite its face. The answer is not only or even mostly that Taiwan is a long-festering wound for the party. Rather, the Chinese Communists know that the fall of Taiwan, while inflicting considerable pain on China, would set the stage for a long-term victory over the United States.

The first long-term consequence of Taiwan's fall would be the weakening of America's friends and the fraying of our alliances around the world. Remember that Douglas MacArthur called Taiwan "an unsinkable aircraft carrier and submarine tender." China would immediately make it so, transforming the "first island chain" from an obstacle to China's ambitions to a springboard. With air and naval bases on Taiwan, China could project power into the Pacific Ocean and the broader world. It would also dominate the vast South China Sea atop which Taiwan sits like a cork in a bottle. And China would exploit our allies' badly shaken confidence in the United States as a security partner.

These strategic advantages would enable China to dominate its neighborhood. Japan would feel particularly vulnerable. Japan is a critical ally and military partner, the cornerstone of our entire defensive strategy in the Pacific since we won World War II. But China would control Japan's access to the South China Sea through which flows an estimated 90 percent of Japan's oil imports and 60 percent of its natural-gas imports. China would also severely threaten Japan's islands, some of which it already claims as its own. Japan would have little choice but to rapidly build up its military or to accommodate Chinese demands—and probably both. Our own military bases in Japan, and our economic and political relationship, would be threatened.

The situation would be worse for other nations, which lack Japan's wealth to support a military buildup. To Taiwan's immediate south, the Philippines would struggle to defend its main islands, to say nothing of the smaller islands claimed by China. In short order, more than a half billon people in the Philippines, Indonesia, Vietnam, Thailand, Malaysia, and other nations in Southeast Asia would fall into a vast Chinese sphere of influence. Unlike Japan's Greater East Asia Co-Prosperity Sphere in World War II or Soviet Russia's Iron Curtain during the Cold War, China wouldn't need to subjugate these nations or govern them by military force. Rather, the Chinese Communist Party could use economic carrots and sticks, along with military threats, to keep them in line. These nations, which include American treaty allies and close partners, would begin to give the United States the cold shoulder to curry favor with China.

Nor would the cascading effects stop there. India could start hedging its bets and appeasing China to avoid further aggression in the Himalayas. An emboldened China would likely seek overseas military bases to project power and safeguard its access to natural resources;

it would find willing partners in the Middle East and Africa, where it's already making inroads. China might also seek allies and bases in Latin America to threaten us in our backyard. Not even Europe would be exempt. Most European countries already refuse to get tough on China's economic warfare and abuse of its own people; as China's global power grows, European leaders won't suddenly grow a backbone.

A second, related consequence of Chinese victory in Taiwan would likely be widespread nuclear proliferation. For eighty years, we have largely limited the spread of nuclear weapons—only nine countries have the bomb today—in part by assuring other nations that they can count on our security guarantees and our nuclear umbrella. But those assurances would be worthless if China took Taiwan. Japan is just a proverbial wrench turn away from nuclear weapons and would likely turn the wrench to protect itself from China. In that case, with nuclear weapons states surrounding it on all sides, South Korea would probably follow suit. Australia might, too. India would surely expand its arsenal to deter Chinese aggression in the Himalayas, but then Pakistan would match India. In this environment, Iran would feel emboldened to race toward a nuclear breakout, which in turn would compel Arab nations to pursue their own nukes. Meanwhile, China would respond by adding even more nuclear weapons, which would likely cause Russia to do the same. In sum, the number of nuclear nations and nuclear weapons would skyrocket if China conquered Taiwan.

As dangers grow and nuclear weapons spread, a third consequence of Taiwan's fall would be the decline of American influence and pro-American sentiment around the world. For decades after World War II, the United States inspired peoples and protected friendly governments from Communist subjugation. But China's extension of its surveillance police state over Taiwan— one of the world's most vibrant democracies—would demoralize our friends and encourage strongmen worldwide. The Chinese Communist Party would crow about the death of the only democracy on Chinese soil, contending more forcefully than ever that democratic freedom isn't suitable for China's historical, cultural, and social conditions. Socialists and dictators across Asia, Africa, and Latin America would press the same case about their nations and seek ideological and military support from China. Pro-American nations would wonder whether they could still count on the United States, and many would start appeasing and kowtowing to China. American rhetoric would ring hollow as our power and influence waned.

After remaking the world's security and political environment, China would have the leverage to impose a final consequence on the United States: long-term economic stagnation and irrelevance. As we saw in chapter 3, the Chinese Communist Party has waged economic world war against America for decades starting from a position of weakness. But once it gains the position of strength by seizing Taiwan, the Chinese Communists will aim to win the war once and for all. China will double down on the economic crimes we've already seen: state-subsidized companies, dumping subsidized goods into foreign markets, intellectual-property theft, expropriation, one-sided tariffs and quotas. What's more, as China acts with impunity, America's erstwhile friends will watch silently lest China target them as well.

And it would get worse: China could compel other nations to employ similar tactics against the United States. It could demand preferential trade terms for itself and harmful terms for us, with the economic leverage and military might to enforce its demands. China might still sell us hundreds of billions of dollars in goods, but only on its terms: no reciprocity, no enforcement of trade agreements, no protections for American workers and businesses.

Over time, China could gradually cut the United States off from East Asia, the largest and fastest-growing economic region in the world. It could close not only its own markets, but also the markets of its economic vassal states to our farmers and manufacturers. In the other direction, China could constrict the supply of critical goods for our economy—from semiconductors to the rare minerals essential to all modern electronics to basic medicines and medical supplies—and insist that other nations do the same. The United States would struggle to reshore and rebuild our manufacturing industry, and China would obstruct all such efforts.

A final blow would be China's demand that other countries stop trading in dollars, which would undermine the dollar's status as the world's reserve currency. That may seem abstract, but it would lead to higher borrowing costs in the United States—both for families buying homes and cars and our government's bloated deficit—lower stock-market values, less investment in the United States, and much weaker sanctions on rogue regimes and terrorists. All of which is China's point, of course: to weaken and impoverish our nation.

Where would it all end? Would China continue its military buildup until it could one day invade and occupy America? Probably not, at least not as long as we maintain our own nuclear forces as the ultimate deterrent. But it wouldn't need to, either. Taiwan in hand, the Chinese Communist Party could gradually but inexorably hollow out American power and curtail our global influence.

Even Henry Kissinger warned deputy national security advisor and China expert Matt Pottinger that a victorious China could turn the United States into "an island off the coast of the world," isolated and separated from former allies and trading partners. That may seem far-fetched, but it really isn't if you look at the facts. The United States has only 4 percent of the world's population and 6 percent of its land. We account for about a quarter of the global economy, but that would decline rapidly after the global depression and supercharged Chinese economic warfare that would follow Taiwan's fall.

Moreover, China doesn't hide these ambitions. According to former national security advisor H. R. McMaster, China's premier, Li Keqiang, told him and President Trump during a state visit to China in 2017 that America would become little more than an economic colony to a dominant China: "the U.S. role in the future global economy would be to provide China with raw materials, agricultural products, and energy to fuel its production of the world's cutting-edge industrial and consumer products." Pottinger also attended the meeting and adds that Li observed that China could also get its commodities from South America, Africa, and the Middle East if the United States didn't acquiesce to Chinese hegemony.

What may seem far-fetched to most Americans are in fact the long-standing ambitions and plans of the Chinese Communists.

*   *   *

China could defeat America in the global struggle for mastery; it all starts and really ends in Taiwan. No one can predict with certainty how a Chinese invasion of Taiwan would end up, especially without knowing how the United States would respond. But however it turns out, it would set off a catastrophic chain of events. The only winning strategy to preserve American primacy is to deter Chinese aggression in the first place.

In 1964, Ronald Reagan told his generation of Americans, "You and I have a rendezvous with destiny. We'll preserve for our children this, the last best hope of man on earth, or we'll sentence them to take the last step into a thousand years of darkness." So, too, is our choice today.

Fortunately, we still have a choice—we still have what George Washington wanted for our nation: command of our own fortunes. China could indeed win, but only if America lets it.

Epilogue

How can we exercise command of our own fortunes and prevail against Communist China? More to the point, how can *you* help? As a private citizen, you can't impose sanctions on Chinese Communists or raise tariffs on Chinese goods—but you can vote for elected officials who will. Ours is still a republic of the people, by the people, and for the people; you and your neighbors can make a difference. Having examined together seven things you can't say about China, let me now suggest seven things you can do in your daily life to help America beat China.

First, stay informed and keep learning about the Chinese Communist Party. Follow news reports about China. Read more books like this one about the Chinese Communist threat. The most potent antidote for Chinese propaganda is the truth.

Second, inform your friends and family—especially your kids—about China. You're probably one of their most trusted sources of information, and if you're passionate, informed, and respectful, they'll listen. Share this book with them. Send them links to news about Communist China's crimes. Encourage them to join you in doing these seven things to beat China. Teach your kids especially the truth about China. The struggle against China will last for a long time, and the next generation needs to know the truth. My two boys are still too young to be exposed to harsh realities such as the Uyghur genocide, but they know that the men who govern China are evil and that we pray for the Chinese people to live in freedom one day.

Third, make China a priority on Election Day, especially in your votes for Congress and the presidency. Vote for candidates who will repeal China's preferential trade status, rebuild our military, combat Chinese influence in America, and crack down on Chinese fentanyl. I stand up to China not only because it's the right thing to do, but also because Arkansans expect it from me; my polling has shown for years that Arkansans strongly oppose China and prioritize it highly among their concerns. Your vote can similarly influence your representatives. Encourage your friends and family to vote on China as well.

Don't forget your state and local elections. Look for candidates who understand the threat of Chinese communism and who will battle it. State and local officials are particularly responsive to you and your concerns because they're closer to you. In Arkansas, for instance, our legislators banned Chinese land purchases and crypto mines because of genuine outcry from their voters.

And stay engaged and hold your elected officials accountable between elections. If politicians break their promises or go soft on China, call and write them. Even better, call and write them before they let you down. Encourage them to get tough on China and praise them when they do. Thank them for working in a bipartisan fashion to stand up to China, as so many Republicans did when we supported Nancy Pelosi's trip to Taiwan in 2022. I promise you that letters, emails, and phone calls to your representatives can make a difference. In my office, we closely track what matters to Arkansans so much that they call or write me. I've seen several bills die because of intense outreach from the folks back home.

In your state and community, you can go a step farther and easily attend government meetings. As we saw in chapter 5, a Chinese company almost built a suspiciously large tower near the sensitive Grand Forks Air Force Base. Local officials celebrated the economic investment and job creation at first. But engaged local citizens began showing up at meetings to oppose the project and ultimately prevailed, after which they broke out into chants of "U.S.A!" You can do the same, for example, if your school board plans to adopt a Communist-influenced curriculum, if your city proposes a sister-city relationship with China, or if your state legislature gives subsidies and tax breaks to Chinese companies.

Fourth, keep your kids and family off Chinese apps. If your child has TikTok on their phone, explain the dangers and delete it. Avoid other Chinese apps like Temu, Alibaba, Shein, WeChat, and Alipay. A few dollars savings or a little extra convenience isn't worth the threat to your family's privacy and data security or the indirect help these apps provide to the Chinese Communists.

Fifth, boycott products made in China as best you can. I know it's not easy, and for some things, it's nearly impossible; decades of mistakes by Washington politicians have limited your choices on a range of goods. No one expects you to throw away your Nike T-shirts or smash your iPhone. My family doesn't, either. But check the label or read the fine print on the website before you buy. If it comes from China, spend a few extra minutes trying to find an alternative.

You can extend the principle beyond products. Don't reward celebrity apologists for the Chinese Communists like Lebron James and John Cena; skip their games, movies, and endorsed products. Do the same for companies like Disney that kowtow to China. If you're a college graduate, tell your alma mater to sever ties with China. If you're in a union, encourage your leaders to divest the pension fund from Chinese investments. If you're a professional who can choose your clients, refuse to do business with Chinese companies or tell your employer you don't want to work on Chinese accounts. Take every opportunity to deny money and legitimacy to the Chinese government.

Sixth, try to buy American when you can. Again, it's

not always possible, thanks to misguided trade policies, but we should reward manufacturers that stay in America. By pulling your family's spending from Chinese companies and directing it to American companies, you can strike a double blow. When you can't find an American alternative, look for non-Chinese options, especially from allied nations like Japan and South Korea. Don't miss a chance to demonstrate your disgust with Chinese communism.

Seventh, pray for the Chinese people, the first and worst victims of the Chinese Communist Party. For more than a century, the Communists have oppressed billions of captive subjects and desecrated Chinese history and culture. Let us pray for an end to their suffering and the end of the Communist regime in Beijing.

Above all, let us also pray for peace and the strength and resolve to preserve the peace.

These seven suggestions aren't the only things you can do, but they won't take much of your time or effort, especially if you care enough about the threat to have read this far. If you keep these seven things in mind, you'll have done more than your part to help defeat this evil empire and curtail its insidious influence in our country. America's greatest strength is now and always has been her people. With your help, I'm confident America will win.

Acknowledgments

As with my earlier books, I want to thank at the outset the people of Arkansas for the honor of serving you in the Senate. Even more than with my previous books, I developed the ideas and gained the experiences discussed in this book as a result of working for you over the last dozen years. I'm grateful for the opportunity and for your continued support.

I'm also grateful for the aid of several capable advisers and assistants. Patrick MacDonnell once again assisted with research and collaborated with me on the manuscript. Brian Colas helped shape the structure of the book and keep it direct, plainspoken, and free of jargon. Doug Coutts and Joni Deoudes continued to keep me on track in the Senate, on the campaign trail, and at home despite the demands of writing a book; Joni also oversaw the Senate's contract-review process. A. J. Schroeder again aided with operations and logistics, and Caroline Tabler again pitched in with the book launch. Patrick McCann assisted with fact-checking.

I'm grateful to several friends who went the extra mile to review the manuscript: Bart Hester, Jonny Hiler, Joe

Kristol, Michael Lamoureux, John Martin, and Brett O'Donnell. Much though they added, the book's contents are of course my responsibility alone, as are any mistakes that slipped by their eagle eyes.

Javelin served again as my agent, and I appreciate the continued support of Keith Urbahn and Matt Latimer.

Sean Desmond was my editor again, this time at Harper. It was good to work again with Sean and good to return to HarperCollins, which published *Sacred Duty*. The concept for this book was Sean's idea; I'm grateful to him for encouraging me to synthesize and elaborate what I'd said and written about the Chinese Communist Party for several years. Sean also sharpened the book's arguments and prose throughout the editorial process. And I appreciate the assistance of his team at Harper, including Jonathan Burnham, Doug Jones, Tina Andreadis, Tom Hopke, Theresa Dooley, Jocelyn Larnick, and David Koral.

I'm most grateful for my family. Cowboy once again served as my writing partner. At sixteen years old, he wasn't as energetic as he once was, but he was still a good companion at my feet during the long writing sessions. We lost him during the editing process, but we'll always cherish his memory. I'll always remember the look in his eyes across three books, which seemed to say, "You need a break and I need a walk." My sons, Gabriel and Daniel, aren't old enough to understand or be exposed to a lot of what's in this book, but they are old enough to know that "bad men rule China" and to pray that the Chinese people will one day live in peace and freedom.

Finally, this book—like everything else in my life—wouldn't have been possible without the love and support of my wife, Anna. I would be fortunate if she merely tolerated the demands of my work in and out of the Senate, including this third book. But she doesn't just tolerate it—she pushes me, encourages me, and backs me to the hilt. Words can't express my gratitude to her, so I'll simply say: I love you, Anna.

Notes on Sources

This book combines history and current events, including my own experience in the U.S. Senate. For the latter, I've used my own recollections, notes, and past writing. For recent events, I've relied on contemporaneous news reporting from customary media sources, including the *Wall Street Journal*, the *Washington Post*, the *New York Times*, the Associated Press, Reuters, Fox, CNN, ABC, CBS, and NBC, among others. Most of this material is widely available through internet search engines.

I didn't arrive in Congress as an expert on China, though I was never confused about the Chinese Communist Party. As I write in chapter 1, I recall watching the news about the Tiananmen Square protests in 1989, thrilling at the bravery of "Tank Man" and the other students, and then feeling dismayed at the crackdown—and confused as to why no one did much of anything about it. I was appalled in 1997 as a student at Harvard when the university invited Jiang Zemin to speak on campus. And I applauded the protesters along the torch-relay route for the 2008 "Genocide Olympics" in Beijing.

During my time in Congress, I've added greater understanding to those instincts. I've benefited from the advice and insights of a large group of peers, advisers, aides, and administration officials. Peter Berkowitz, Dan Blumenthal, Mike Gallagher, Robert Lighthizer, Aaron MacLean, Robert O'Brien, Matt Pottinger, Alex Wong, and Miles Yu especially contributed to my thinking about the threat from Chinese communism. Many years of hearings, briefings, and reading on the Senate Intelligence Committee, Senate Armed Services Committee, and House Foreign Affairs Committee have also informed my views. I'm also grateful for the firsthand testimony of Uyghurs, Tibetans, Hong Kongers, and other victims of Chinese communism; their witness is a solemn reminder of the stakes in this struggle.

Below, I've provided a more detailed list of the specific books, articles, and other sources I consulted for each chapter.

Prologue

I relied on my own experiences and recollections about the early days of the coronavirus pandemic, along with contemporaneous news reports. I would prefer, as you probably would, to forget those days, but we shouldn't forget the treachery of the Chinese Communist Party, nor the complicity of its apologists.

I: China Is an Evil Empire

For the history of the Chinese Communist Party, I consulted Jung Chang and Jon Halliday's *Mao*, Julia Lovell's *Maoism*, and Frank Dikötter's *China After Mao*. These books provide detailed research and moral clarity for anyone chronicling the Chinese Communist Party's long history of murder and oppression.

I drew upon open-source reporting, my experiences in the Senate, and discussions with experts like Matt Pottinger and Miles Yu for the party's more recent crimes. I referred to Chun Han Wong's *Party of One* and Adrian Geiges and Stefan Aust's *Xi Jinping*, using these impressive biographies of China's dictator for background and quotations in this chapter and elsewhere in the book.

Kai Strittmatter's *We Have Been Harmonized* and Josh Chin and Liza Lin's *Surveillance State* examine China's high-tech and brutal police state, as do several reports by Freedom House. The China Tribunal and the Victims of Communism Memorial Foundation have exposed the gruesome reports of Chinese organ harvesting. I was particularly moved by Nury Turkel's *No Escape*, which documents the horrors of China's concentration camps and genocide of the Uyghur people.

II: China Is Preparing for War

The Chinese Communist Party has a long and well-documented history of aggression. I found these books particularly helpful: Julia Lovell's *Maoism*, David Shambaugh's *China's Leaders*, Jung Chang and Jon Halliday's *Mao*, Margaret MacMillan's *Nixon and Mao*, Michael Lind's *Vietnam: The Necessary War*, and Ian Easton's *The Chinese Invasion Threat*. For China's recent aggression and foreign policy, I consulted Michael Beckley and Hal Brands's *Danger Zone*, Rush Doshi's *The Long Game*, Robert Gates's *Exercise of Power*, and Peter Martin's *China's Civilian Army*.

The best source for China's military buildup is the Pentagon's annual report *Military and Security Developments Involving the People's Republic of China*. These public reports provide invaluable and reliable unclassified information on the size and sophistication of the Chinese military, along with analysis of recent Chinese aggression. These reports also form the basis for periodic briefings and hearings at the Senate Armed Services Committee. Open-source reporting occasionally reveals alarming news about China's military buildup, notably suggesting that China's leaders want the world to know what they're doing. Finally, several unclassified war games between China and Taiwan produce unhappy but informative results; I found most helpful the war games from the House Select Committee on the Chinese Communist Party, the Center for a New American Security, and RAND.

III: China Is Waging Economic World War

I have studied, spoken, and written about the Chinese Communist Party's economic crimes for many years in the Senate. A good starting point is my report from 2021, *Beat China: Targeted Decoupling and the Economic Long War.* For insights into the history and structure of the Chinese economy, I also drew from Frank Dikötter's *China After Mao*, which explains the true intentions and strategy behind the party's modern economic planning.

Several authors have catalogued China's economic bullying and aggression against other nations, especially the United States. Former U.S. Trade Representative Robert Lighthizer sounded the alarm early in his writing and public service; I have benefited from our conversations over the years and from his excellent book, *No Trade Is Free.* I also consulted Bethany Allen's *Beijing Rules*, Joanna Chiu's *China Unbound*, Adrian Geiges and Stefan Aust's *Xi Jinping*, Peter Martin's *China's Civilian Army*, and Michael Beckley and Hal Brands's *Danger Zone.* I relied on Jonathan Hillman's *The Emperor's New Road* for information and anecdotes related to China's Belt and Road Initiative.

IV: China Has Infiltrated
Our Society

This chapter draws heavily on open-source information, yet the dots aren't often connected. For example, you would probably realize, if you reflected on it, that Hollywood hasn't produced a movie with a Chinese villain since the late 1990s. And it's no secret that all major news networks (except Fox) are owned by or affiliated with a Hollywood studio. Same thing with the NBA's deep ties to China. Now that you know the backstory and implications, you can connect the dots when these stories appear in the news.

I also relied on several books for deeper examination of these issues. Erich Schwartzel's *Red Carpet* thoroughly exposes China's influence over American celebrities and movie studios. I also drew from Bethany Allen's *Beijing Rules*, Clive Hamilton and Mareike Ohlberg's *Hidden Hand*, Peter Schweizer's *Red-Handed*, Peter Martin's *China's Civilian Army*, and Josh Chin and Liza Lin's *Surveillance State* for additional examples of how China has infiltrated and influenced the news media, corporate America, and higher education.

Finally, the Department of Education and the House Select Committee on the Chinese Communist Party have revealed extensive Chinese influence over American higher education and high finance.

V: China Has Infiltrated
Our Government

Much of this chapter comes from my own work in the
Senate and from experiences in politics. Suffice it to
say, the Chinese Communist Party doesn't view me as
a promising target; on the contrary, they slapped sanctions on me in 2020. But I see how China operates in
the Washington influence industry, and I hear stories
from like-minded acquaintances who want to expose
and curtail Chinese influence. I also have benefited from
conversations with veterans of our intelligence agencies,
who must remain unnamed for obvious reasons.

Department of Justice charging documents, which
are usually in the public domain, provide helpful insight
into Chinese techniques, as do contemporaneous news
reports covering these cases. Alex Joske's *Spies and Lies*
offers a concise history of Chinese spycraft and influence
operations in America.

In detailing the power of the New China Lobby and
the scope of Chinese influence in state and local governments, I also consulted Isaac Stone Fish's *America Second*,
Bethany Allen's *Beijing Rules*, Peter Schweizer's *Red-
Handed*, and Aaron Friedberg's *Getting China Wrong*. I
relied on my own recollection and conversations with
friends and associates to recount China's activities in my
own state.

VI: China Is Coming for Our Kids

I have worked extensively in the Senate on the threat of TikTok and, in this chapter, I draw upon those experiences and on the work of the House Select Committee on the Chinese Communist Party. The *Wall Street Journal* and the *New York Times* have also published thorough and deep investigative reports into the dark side of Tik-Tok. I took data from Pew Research and an analysis of TikTok hashtags from the Network Contagion Research Institute and Rutgers University.

I consulted three reports in particular to expose China's influence on our kids' schools: the Senate Permanent Subcommittee on Investigations' report *China's Impact on the U.S. Education System*, the National Association of Scholars' report *Corrupting the College Board: Confucius Institutes and K–12 Education*, and the Parents Defending Education's report *Little Red Classrooms: China's Infiltration of American K–12 Schools*. All three reports provide damning evidence of China's disturbing campaign to influence our primary and secondary education systems.

To tell the story of the Reverse Opium War, Stephen R. Platt's *Imperial Twilight*, Jung Chang and Jon Halliday's *Mao*, and Julia Lovell's *Maoism* were especially helpful. The House Select Committee on the Chinese Communist Party's report *The CCP's Role in the Fen-*

tanyl Crisis establishes China's culpability for our nation's worst drug epidemic, as does Ben Westhoff's book *Fentanyl, Inc.*

VII: China Could Win

As I started this book, I was surprised at how little others had written about the logical and likely consequences of a Chinese conquest of Taiwan. Many smart and trenchant books and articles make only passing and ominous reference to it or merely assume it would be very harmful, without detailed explanation. Thus, I wanted to elaborate exactly why and how the fall of Taiwan would be catastrophic to America's vital national interests—or, as General Douglas MacArthur put it, why "the domination of [Taiwan] by an unfriendly power would be a disaster of utmost importance to the United States."

I benefited here especially from several conversations with Matt Pottinger. He subsequently published "The Taiwan Catastrophe," an excellent article coauthored by Andrew Erickson and Gabriel Collins in *Foreign Affairs*. This piece also lays out the awful consequences of Chinese control over Taiwan. The article is now a chapter in *The Boiling Moat*, a book edited by Pottinger that sounds the alarm about the threat to Taiwan and offers "urgent steps" to defend the island. The Pacific

Forum has published a similar compilation of expert analysis, *The World After Taiwan's Fall*, another helpful source for this chapter.

Finally, I cited economic analysis from Bloomberg Economics, statistics from Hal Brands and Michael Beckley's *Danger Zone*, an anecdote from H. R. McMaster's *Battlegrounds*, and analysis from Michael Sobolik's *Countering China's Great Game* and Ian Easton's *The Chinese Invasion Threat*.

Index

About the Author

Tom Cotton is a United States senator from Arkansas and the bestselling author of *Sacred Duty* and *Only the Strong*. He served in Iraq with the 101st Airborne Division and in Afghanistan with a Provincial Reconstruction Team. Between combat tours, he served with the United States Army's 3rd Infantry Regiment ("The Old Guard") at Arlington National Cemetery. His military decorations include the Bronze Star, the Combat Infantryman Badge, and the Ranger Tab. He served one term in the House of Representatives before his election to the Senate. A graduate of Harvard College and Harvard Law School, he is married to Anna and they have two sons, Gabriel and Daniel.